How To
STOP SABOTAGING
Your
SUCCESS

(and get what you want guilt free)

All the Best

Introducing

DR SPACE™

HOW TO STOP SABOTAGING YOUR SUCCESS
(and get what you want guilt free)

First published 2001 by
design4success™ publications
The Gardens, Sisland, Loddon, Norwich NR14 6EE

ISBN 0-9540783-0-6

British Library Cataloguing in Publication Data
A catalogue record for this book is available from the British Library

Typeset by
The Cyber~Press, Southolt Road, Worlingworth, Suffolk

Printed and bound by
Print Wright Ltd, Ipswich, Suffolk

About The Author

Clive Hall founded and ran his own independent financial advice business for 30 years after serving in the Royal Air Force for seven years as an electronic technician.

As a financial adviser he was also responsible for the recruitment, training, motivation and management of a 200 strong sales force.

His natural and infectious enthusiasm for realising human potential led to requests to speak in front of sales forces from other companies in and outside the financial services world.

Having sold his financial services business he now runs **design4success**™, a training and business consultancy and is retained by several client companies and private businesses to advise them on personal development coaching, training and sales strategies.

Initial consultations are free and Clive has created a suite of seminars on a variety of subjects including time management, prosperity, sales techniques, people skills and stress avoidance all of which can be modified to build bespoke courses for client companies and businesses.

Clive is a Regional Director of The Consultants Development Network (formerly the British Business Consultants and Trainers Academy (BBCTA).

Having retired from playing rugby after nearly 50 seasons Clive is utilising his spare energy by involvement with a Relationship marketing company which he sees as the business of the future for budding entrepreneurs.

Clive and his wife Bren also have their own property business and devote time to their charity, Give A Man A Net (GAMAN), when not working in their one and a half acre garden at their home in Norfolk.

He is already working on his next book on personal development and also has the first draft of a novel which he hopes to see published in the not too distant future.

Acknowledgements

Anyone who has written, or tried to write, a book knows that it is not a solo effort.

This modest volume would not have reached production without the valued and timely support of many people. My heartfelt thanks to them, not in any particular order, go to:

Peter Thompson and Andy Gilbert of The Consultants Development Network for their encouragement and example.

Tony Brown of Lead The Field in whose e-zine of the same name, Chapter 1 of my book appeared as an article. Thanks also to his readers who contacted me with kind words of appreciation. Tony also provided me with some of the data on Alexander The Great and Gandhi.

Sue Austin who read my first draft and pointed out not only where I had used the wrong words and the occasions where I had used the right words but made little sense.

To Eric Cross, my English master at The Cedars School, who always appreciated my efforts in his classes.

To David Marler and his team at Chase Financial Services Ltd. who were my first paying clients and with whom it has been a pleasure to coach. It was great to see the growth and development of their knowledge, attitude, skills and habits as we worked through and fine tuned the DR SPACE™ process for the very first time.

To Linda Foulston of Cyber~Press, who made my words into a book, for her knowledge of the world of printing, her ideas for the cover and her introduction to Print

Wright Ltd. Last but by no means least to Gill Robinson at Print Wright who resisted my urgency and insisted that they take the time they needed to produce the book properly.

You all contributed. Any errors are mine and mine alone.

To Bren

Contents

Introduction

I have written this book because I firmly believe that success does not happen by accident and that it is available to each and every one of us.

It took me many years to realise this and I wanted others to be aware that it is possible to have great things in life without feeling guilty about having them.

I know now that achieving anything is just a process, so this book can be regarded as a turn key manual for success.

We all make mistakes throughout our lives and if I have any qualification for assuming the role of author of a personal development book it is because I have probably made more mistakes than most. In fact I have made some of them twice but I suppose this only taught me whatever lesson was to be learned in a slightly different way.

Whatever your current situation it is the sum product of your influences and experiences to date. They have made the unique person that is you.

Through out this book I have illustrated points with my own experiences in the hope that you will be able to take them for your own without having to pay the price which I have done.

I have acknowledged the influences in my own personal growth in as far as I recognise them and if they were not the original source then my apologies are given and I will make amends in subsequent reprints should I be so advised.

Aristotle, one of my heroes, was perhaps the first person to promulgate the concept of cause and effect.

I sincerely hope that reading this book will be the cause of effecting your life to become what you want it to be.

If it achieves this then I know that not only will your life be better than it is now but so will the lives of every one with whom you come into contact.

To change our future we have to change ourselves.

Change does not have to be a painful process and I hope reading my book and enjoying your future will bring you as much fun, pleasure and satisfaction as I gained from writing it.

All The Best

Clive Hall

The Mexican Fisherman

Peter Thompson first told me this story.

An American management consultant was on vacation in Mexico and he fell into conversation at the small jetty of the village he was staying in for the night.

The Mexican fisherman had just come in with a boat full of delicious fish he had caught.

He asked the fisherman if he would be making another trip that day.

The fisherman told him that he would not. Indeed he intended, as always after having a few glasses of wine and a spot of lunch with his friends, to spend some time with his wife and children when they came home from school.

Later in the evening he would have another glass of wine with his wife and have some supper while watching the sun go down over the bay.

The management consultant said that he could see how the fisherman could transform his life and make a fortune. With his guidance the fisherman could get another boat and hire a man to fish from it. After a while they could build it up to a fleet and corner the market.

They could open a canning plant, go into export and maybe move the whole operation away from the village.

They would have to raise venture capital but the eventual flotation and sale would make them both rich.

The fisherman asked how long all of this would take and was told maybe fifteen to twenty years.

He then asked what would he do after that.

With great delight the management consultant explained how he could retire to a small peaceful village, spend the morning doing a bit of fishing from the boat he would own. He could go on to have a glass of wine or two and some lunch with his friends. He could go home to see his wife, have time to see his family and spend the evening in leisure.

I repeat this story to point out that success is a personal thing. What may be success to one person may be regarded as failure by another.

My aim in writing this book is to help you identify what your version is and to show you how you can have it.

CHAPTER 1
It's Never too late

"You are absolutely mad", said most of my friends.

For thirty years I had run my own Independent Financial Services Business. Although there had been ups and downs, like any business, it had been very successful providing us with a high standard of living, great holidays and new cars every two years.

Some of the downs were not too good. There were years when the cash flow was negative and survival was only maintained by increasing the working capital by heavy borrowing.

There was one year when I took no salary whatsoever. For the entire period the staff came first when it came to pay day and I often wondered what it would be like to work for someone else and let them take the pressures.

It may sound stupid not to have realised before but one day it came to me that the purpose of a business was to provide a living for its owner. Instead, I was only working to make sure that my business survived and my staff were employed..

Now here I was having sold up at the age of fifty eight without a job. Perhaps my friends were right. But I didn't think so. What I felt was a sense of freedom. No more regulations. No more staff problems. No more traffic queues.

There were no overheads to find even if business was down and above all I had a glorious feeling which came from knowing that I could do whatever I chose.

Having made the decision it gradually sank in that perhaps I should have done it years ago.

Then came the secondary thought, "Had I left it too late?".

What if I couldn't earn a living somehow? The papers are always running stories about thousands being made redundant and how difficult it is to get a job when over fifty.

I had always sympathised with the people I had read about who discovered they were on the scrap heap and unemployable because of their age. What a waste of experience and maturity !

It takes an age to gain the knowledge and the wrinkles of any job and I was baffled why employers should feel this way.

I had not had a job interview for forty years and I certainly wasn't going to start now. I wasn't going to let someone sell me the idea that I was past it – whatever "it" was.

Maybe it was because I had played rugby for 48 seasons and been told for half of them that I was too old to play that I was not prepared to take the valuation of others as to my self worth.

I had read somewhere that your value to others is determined by what you can give them and I knew I had a lot to give to someone – but what? Self-examination is never a bad thing. A quiet time to ponder the past, the present and the future clarifies issues.

What had I enjoyed the most about my business? How had I enjoyed earning money? What had I not enjoyed? What were my talents and skills as I had only my basic education and what the RAF had taught me about electronics.

What did I know and what was my attitude to life and my values? What mistakes had I made and what could I learn from them? Who could learn from my experience and who would pay for it?

My conclusions were:-

1.   I knew how to run a successful business.

2.   I enjoyed teaching and coaching people.

3. I liked the idea of building a business from scratch and with a low capital requirement.

4. My enthusiasm rubbed off on others.

5. I liked a good financial return on my efforts.

6. I had had enough of staff employment, high capital investment and having to report to a regulator.

7. I liked communicating knowledge through writing and speaking, whether the speaking was on a one to one or group basis.

8. I had made a million mistakes but had learned from them and survived them.

9. I wanted to improve myself further — and knew I had to learn some new skills.

10. I should have done this exercise years ago.

It became obvious that if I could find a market for coaching and training, either businesses or individuals, I could satisfy all my needs, cut out my frustrations and make money.

There are many definitions of success and so there should be, for success is a very personal thing. What is wanted by one person may never be wanted by another.

And there was my business!!

Every one wants success in some form or another and I would help them capture it. There had to be hundreds if not thousands of people who would welcome assistance.

They might not even have defined their personal version of success, and if they had, they may have had no idea about how to go and get it.

Perhaps they did not have the courage to go for it or perhaps they had thought like I had that "It is too late to change".

I knew I could help people and businesses through the process of change and how to design their success.

Now I had a name for my new venture "design4success™" It said it all — or so I thought.

There is an old army saying, "Reconnaissance is seldom wasted". I decided to research the training, consulting and personal motivation world. I discovered that there were several businesses doing what I intended to do and doing it very well in most cases.

An incredible discovery I made was that people were willing to share their ideas.

Determined to learn from the leaders the best way to exploit my position I set out to read, listen to and meet with any one from whom I could learn and gain knowledge.

It was Peter Thompson, founder of the British Business Consultants and Trainers Academy, (Now the Consultants Development Network), who asked me –

"Clive, Why design4success™?"

My immediate response was – "Because it doesn't happen by accident".

In an incredible flash I now had a blueprint laid out before me of my new business venture. Now, I could enjoy the rest of my working life helping others to design their own success.

Design it they must, for it doesn't happen by accident.

I have an expanding and profitable new business which I enjoy. It is already providing me with a better income and less stress and effort than my previous business. I have great satisfaction from seeing my clients achieving, developing and reaping the rewards they have always dreamed of.

I have excluded negative relationships from my life and enjoy more time with Bren, my wife, and our family and our best friends. We take more and better time off yet achieve more when we work.

Our finances and investments like our health and fitness are improved and get better on a daily basis.

Some of our time is given to our charity GAMAN.

The greatest benefit of all is an incredible sense of balance which enables all aspects of life to be enjoyed and celebrated in a guilt free way.

As we achieve more in a shorter time I find it necessary to constantly reset my goals and when I am doing this I always hear myself asking "Why didn't you do all this before?".

The short answer is I didn't know how to.

And that is why this book came into existence.

It is a turnkey manual which you can use to get what you want out of life —— guilt free.

You can use it to achieve things you may never have thought possible.

You can use it to help yourself and others reach heights you once thought out of reach.

You can use it to design your success and make it happen because it doesn't happen by accident.

One other thing ———

——— It is never too late.

Let's get started.

CHAPTER 2
Reinventing yourself

There comes a time in the life of most people when the thought occurs that things need to change.

I was listening to Nathan Rix one day and he said "If you keep doing what you have always done you will get what you have always got".

Later on I heard a definition of insanity.

"Doing the same thing and expecting the outcome to be different".

But we all do it. I often smile to myself when I hear someone taking a photograph say they will just take another one in case the first doesn't come out. They snap happily away without changing anything at all which means to me that they will either have two identical good shots or two identical bad ones.

If you want to get some changes in your life then these changes are going to need to be initiated by you.

The question arises as to why, if you know what changes you need to bring about, you have not done it already?

Maybe you think you have not got the talent you need. Maybe you feel you have a lack of the necessary skills. Is it not having the contacts that is holding you back? How is your confidence or do you feel you need capital to get on the road to success?

Is it a fundamental problem of not even knowing what success is for you?

You would not be alone if the prospect of success actually is a frightening situation strange as that concept may sound.

Nelson Mandela in his acceptance speech of 1993 said:

"Our greatest fear is not that we are inadequate. Our deepest fear is that we are powerful beyond measure. It is our light, not our darkness, that most frightens us. We ask ourselves, "Who am I to be brilliant, or just talented, or fabulous?". Actually, who are you not to be?".

Whatever you define or will come to define as your personal version of success you must be assured that whatever you want can be yours.

We often look with envy at people who have what we want and resign our selves to the fact that such success can never be ours.

This is a big mistake.

Whatever you want can be yours and what is more you can have it without taking it away from any one else.

This may seem an insupportable statement but I promise you that during the course of this book I will show you that this is the case. Once you see this you will be surprised that what you want will change. When you realise that you can get anything you start to become choosy and you may find, as I did, that your wish list changes quite a bit.

Have you ever changed your mind? Of course you have.

Well that is what you are going to have to do if you want to change your life.

You will need to change your mind set.

You may need to change how you think, what you believe, what you know, what you can do and indeed your attitude to many things.

Only by changing these things will you get different results and that is the aim of this book. To get results which you have not so far experienced.

Robert Louis Stevenson said, **"Worthwhile folks don't just happen. You aren't born worthwhile. You are born with the possibilities of becoming worthwhile. Your job is to discover and develop the man or woman you ought to be"**.

You will reinvent yourself into the sort of person who is capable of gaining the rewards you would like for doing the sort of things you would like to do.

Although I use the term reinvent the fact is that you don't have to be fixed because you are not broken. All you need to do is be better at being you.

One word of warning: if these changes are to be large ones then they will not happen over night.

The largest vessels afloat, the massive oil tankers, do not have a high rate of acceleration. Once they are up to speed however they can only change direction in small incremental stages due to their built up momentum.

We fail to realise that as human beings we build up a similar kind of momentum, gained piece by piece over many years. Should we wish to change direction at a later stage we have to overcome this momentum. Because it has taken a time to acquire this momentum we are unconscious of it as momentum. As it takes effort to make the change we misinterpret the momentum we have gained as inertia. We think we are at rest and must apply effort in order to get moving.

The fact is if we are moving steadily in the wrong direction we must, like the oil tanker, make small changes to our course otherwise we will finish up in a place we had not intended.

A few years ago I learned the secret of overcoming the inherent tendency to continue on the same course, to stay in the same old comfortable rut.

First recognise that sensible rule:

If you keep on doing what you have always done you will get what you have always got.

Second, be like that oil tanker:

Make many small changes to achieve big changes.

In other words take baby steps. Think about this.

Even the Olympic 100 metres Champion, the fastest human being on the planet, once had to learn how to walk and take baby steps.

Later in the book, in fact in the next chapter, we will be looking at the various areas of your life where you may want to change the way you operate. In each of these areas you may decide that you want to have some form of improvement. You may decide that the way you are doing something could be done in a different way so that you get a different result: a better way so that you get better results.

You may wish to become a different person as regards that particular life part. That is what you will do. You will discover why you operate the way you do and what is stopping you doing things in a different way.

One thing before we really get started.

You are to measure yourself in the future against how you are today. You will see many changes. That is what you are seeking.

You will be identifying and emulating some role models and it will be natural for you to try and measure yourself against them but that is not the task.

You are to measure your self against yourself. You are to improve in the areas you choose.

It doesn't matter if you are not the best in the world at anything as long you are the best you can be.

Every one has greatness within them regardless of deficiencies which you may feel you have. These deficiencies do not matter. It is the good and fine points which make you into the person you are. Use them and develop them to create a better you.

If your goal is to be the best in the world you can only achieve it by being the best you can be. If you were to fail in that ultimate goal but still had maximised your full potential you would be a success.

Put no limits on what you wish to achieve. Aim high and work towards it with a plan.

As you learn more about the person you are and have become, you will identify the changes you will want to make in order to become the new you. You will see theses changes as several small changes which will be easily absorbed into your daily life until you become the person you want to be. The person who is capable of achieving all that you would like to achieve if you were not the person you are now.

In other words you will have reinvented yourself.

Chapter 3
Getting a Mentor

My Grandfather, a man for whom I had the most tremendous respect, once gave me some advice which shaped my life for the next fifty years.

He told me, "Never be number one. Always be number two and that way you will not be knocked off your perch and you can always improve if you want to".

Now I may have got it wrong or I may have misunderstood but for some reason it made a deep impression and was a main guiding principle in my life.

The problem was that it had a very bad effect on my achievements.

Whenever I was in a new area, such as a new subject at school, starting a new project or learning a new skill I got off to a great start. I was often the best of the bunch.

Once the results of the first test came out and I discovered I was number one I rapidly applied the hand brake and subsequently under performed in order to ensure that I was not at the top any more.

This attitude also influenced other aspects of my behaviour. It made me get very close to any goal I had set but made me cease action at the last moment so that I subsequently had to rush to finish the project at the eleventh hour.

Of course it was not the only principle in my life. Our beliefs, our paradigms, our rules of operation are gradually acquired as we grow. If we are fortunate we discard rules which are bad for us and replace them with better ones.

In the great book, I'm OK–You're OK by Thomas A. Harris M.D. (Arrow Books) it is suggested that we have a great recording system in our heads which records not only everything which happens to us but also every feeling and emotion which we are experiencing when those things happen.

The problem is that when faced with a similar situation later in life we may not recognise the similarity between the two situations but we will sub consciously react in the same emotional way we did when we were in the first situation.

So if as a tiny child, helpless, frustrated by being in an uncomfortable position we resolved the problem by screaming and throwing our toys out of the pram we may react in the same way later in life.

If as a teenager we are given some instruction by our parents which we feel to be very unfair so that we rebelled, we may do so again if someone, say a boss or manager or even the government, tells us to do something.

As we mature we learn, if we are fortunate, how to act appropriately and to make our own minds up about what are the correct rules of life.

It takes a lot of self examination to understand that how we deal with life today is very much a function of our early formative years.

For instance at school we are taught (and then tested) that it is wrong to make mistakes.

It is not wrong to make mistakes. It is wrong not to learn from our mistakes. If we make a mistake it probably means we are in uncharted territory. We are in unfamiliar ground.

When we were born we had a fear of falling and a fear of loud noises. We played happily, making mistakes and learning.

Only later in life did we learn that we must not make mistakes or we would pay a penalty.

It is this fear which is one of the most self limiting factors today causing millions never to attempt the unfamiliar and so never realise their full potential.

Sometimes we would rather not do something than attempt it and make a mistake.

Think about completing your tax return. You know it must be done but you know that there are penalties to pay if it is completed inaccurately. Subconsciously we therefore decide to delay starting it so as to delay the possibility of making errors and getting a "3/10. SEE ME".

We are also conditioned at an early age by insensitive criticism.

At school you may perhaps have been going down with a cold during a maths class and missed a vital point meaning that your homework scored a low mark.

Your teacher may have called you a failure and even said you are no good at maths.

This damaging statement would have put into your subconscious mind the fact that you were a failure, no good at maths and thus conditioning you to always perform accordingly.

Had the criticism been that on this occasion your homework was not up to standard and that with a little extra tuition it would be possible to understand the lesson and thus be able to apply it in the future for higher marks a different conditioning would have resulted.

There were teachers at my school who told me I was good at the subjects they taught and others who told me I was bad at what they taught.

They were all correct but not for the reason they thought. I performed to their expectation of me and more importantly to my own expectations as conditioned by them.

After I left school and when I started to form my own opinions of what I was good at I found that in fact I was a lot better and more capable than I believed in the areas where I had been told I had no talent and that I would never be any good.

Of course my opinions were also the opinions of people whom I admired and respected.

As adults we are influenced by others but at least we should have the maturity to be able to select people whose values are congruent with our own as role models.

So I decided that what I needed was a mentor. Someone who would help me develop my strengths and help me deal with my weaknesses. It had to be someone who I respected and whose example I could follow in every situation.

Several people came to mind but the first thing to do was to carry out an honest self audit of my self to identify what I believed to be my strengths and weaknesses.

Being honest with your self is not as easy as may be thought. As I attempted my audit I became aware that so many influences had made me a multi-faceted person. Some of my characteristics seemed to be desirable but others certainly needed to be curtailed or modified.

Every coin has two sides and I realised that what was needed was a system whereby I could retain and even boost my self confidence yet reduce any arrogance in my personality. I wanted to become more self interested yet I did not want to lose my concern for other people.

I yearned for more holidays and relaxation yet the work ethic was ingrained in me with a fair dose of guilt packed in my vacation suitcase.

Who should I choose as my mentor? Who had all the attributes I could strive to gain? Who was my perfect mentor?

It dawned on me that there was no one person I could look up to on every occasion.

If only there was someone who had all the strengths of my heroes and none of their weaknesses. Such a person would be ever present and available to guide me, to remind me when I was going astray, to encourage me when things went badly, to help me keep a balance in my life and to help me develop compassion, humour, enthusiasm and worthwhile goals.

Where was he?

CHAPTER 4
Ambition

Are we born to our destiny or do we make it?

Certainly as human beings we have choice over our goals. We are free to decide what we want to achieve in our brief lives.

I suppose like most people I have a latent wish to achieve something. Small boys and for all I know small girls come out of the cinema wanting to be the star of the film. Among my list of careers I considered were:

Polar Explorer, Pioneer, Space Ship Pilot, Surgeon, Fighter Pilot, Bomber Pilot, Artist, Submarine Captain, Master Criminal, Top Detective, Famous Military Leader, Top Athlete, Rancher, Newspaper Magnate, Escaping Prisoner of War, Film Star, Scientist, Prime Minister, Super Hero, Discoverer and Secret Agent.

The glory, the place in history were all very attractive but then there seemed to be an awful lot of inconvenience tied to most of these roles.

A wild imagination can visualise the public admiration and recognition bestowed on the returning hero but it can also visualise the dangers and discomfort experienced in the adventure.

I entered into a pact with two of my eight year old friends to visit the moon one day. One of my chums said he would only go if his Mum could come along as well. I learned fairly early that if you let other people influence you in your wishes for the future you could abandon them before they even get on to the drawing board, let alone off it.

The education system is not geared to develop super heroes. Caped Crusader skills were never on the agenda at any of my schools. When

I had my career interview at school and expressed an interest in becoming a fighter pilot I was steered firmly into applying for a position as a Cadet in the Metropolitan Police.

I did this and was accepted but I never took the position and later joined the Royal Air Force as a Radar Technician. I often wonder if I had been encouraged to follow through on my original dream how my life may have been different.

You may have been fortunate as I was in having at least one parent, in my case my mother, who believed that their progeny would be capable of filling the highest role in any field of endeavour. Any flight of fancy was possible to achieve. This encouragement served to only increase the ambition to be or do something worthwhile.

My more practical father would always ask searching questions as to how I intended to save the human race from impending disaster. The desire to go to the moon out weighed the practical consideration of where the space ship would come from until Dad raised it.

Having spoken to so many people over the years who have unrealised ambitions I now know that ambition should never be crushed in any way. I also learned that the majority of children coming out of the cinema inspired to do great things gradually lose that ambition and settle for smaller and smaller goals.

On every tombstone are two dates with a line between them. The dates are unimportant. It is what the line stands for that is the sum of the life, the achievements gained between the dates.

So in carrying out my self audit I discovered ambition was not dead and that the retention of gigantic goals would at least possibly result in the achievement of large goals.

Who would be my mentor. Who, when I came out of the cinema would say "Go for it!"?

What sort of person had the vision to see a goal which would inspire others to follow him?

Was there any one, alive or dead, who had such a huge goal that any difficulty would seem small in comparison? If this person existed did they reach their goal and did they lead the way when it seemed impossible to go any further?

If I could get someone like this to advise and encourage me when I was setting out on a new venture then surely I too could achieve something worthwhile.

There must be few ambitions as large as to conquer the world. In history there have been several leaders with this goal and some of them have been anti heroes.

Alexander the Great stands out as someone who from an early age knew his destiny and must be in the all time top ten of ambitious people. If he were to be my mentor would he provide the bolster I needed in times of self doubt? Would he provide that essential question of "Why not?" when I proposed some outlandish scheme?

I decided to find out a bit more about him and to see if he would fit the bill of mentor.

ALEXANDER THE GREAT (356–323 BC)

King of Macedonia, great military commander, acknowledged leader of men, builder of a great empire and seeker of truth and knowledge. Alexander was all this and more despite the fact that he died at the young age of 32.

His twin ambitions were a desire to conquer the World, as far as it was then known, and to amass "All knowledge".

Alexander was accompanied on his campaigns by teams of scientists who regularly sent back research data to Aristotle, a previous tutor of his at the Academy in Athens, who was a student of Plato, who in turn had been a student of Socrates.

It is said that when Julius Caesar, at age 40, saw a statue of Alexander, he wept because he hadn't then begun to control his world and yet Alexander had accomplished all his great works and died by age 32!

As a personal hero and role model, Alexander chose Achilles, from Homer's 'Iliad', written back in the 8th century BC and he carried copies of both Homer's 'Iliad' and 'Odyssey' with him at all times during his campaigns, for inspiration.

Alexander's razor sharp intellect and ability to analyse a problem in order to extract its solution marked him out as extraordinary and was the key to both his success on the field of battle and in holding together an empire after he'd built it.

The loyalty he commanded in his troops was absolute, and always by consent. His men claimed that they would follow him to the ends of the earth, and they did. He shared their disappointments as well as their successes and he always led by example, from the front.

During the eight years of his empire building, his troops followed him faithfully, for over 30,000 miles, mostly on foot. A better demonstration of loyalty would be hard to find.

Alexander's courage and prowess on the field of battle has been documented many times, however, it is worth mentioning that in his campaign against Darius, King of Persia, he showed a very early example of psychological warfare.

Although the Persian army was many times greater than his own, Alexander perceived that Darius was not personally a very courageous man. With this mind, he set about creating a 'spearhead' formation of his finest troops, headed it up himself and rushed straight for Darius the king, forcing him from the battlefield, thus totally demoralising the whole Persian army.

He'd literally 'psyched' them out !

In 331 BC, Alexander founded the city of Alexandria in Egypt as well as twelve other cities of the same name, many of which survive today, although their names have been corrupted over time.

His conquests were distinguished by the fact that he preferred to integrate with the local populations rather than simply dominate them. He always attempted to meld cultures together rather than vanquish whole races before the sword, as had been the practice of other empire builders both before him and since.

Alexandria, in Egypt, was to become a great centre of trade and cultural influence, boasting a library of more than 500,000 books which constituted most of the knowledge then available to Mankind. It attracted artists, writers and scientists from all around the world. Both Euclid and Archimedes studied there.

Ptolemy, one of Alexander's generals, was to take over the reins of this empire at his death in 323 BC and go on to develop Alexandria as a centre of learning that flourished and benefited the world for more than 350 years.

Alexander gave away the hoards of gold and silver that he took from the Persians to his veteran soldiers, loyal commanders and religious institutions, releasing vast wealth into the empire.

Above all, his real legacy was his example as an intelligent and compassionate leader.

Here then was my mentor who when I proposed some endeavour would respond favourably and encourage me to see it through.

When I asked Alexander if he would do this for me I am sure I heard "Why not?".

Something to do now

Think of a hero who would encourage you to go for what you want.

CHAPTER 5
Faith and Humility

The say all idols have feet of clay and Alexander the Great seems to be no exception.

As a mentor who encourages and will accept any of my dreams as a target he is supreme.

The only problem is that his faith in his own ability, contagious as it is, can come over as a bit arrogant. Not only that, although he is fanatical about the welfare of his soldiers and horses he is a little mean when it comes to being kind to his enemies during battle. Then again I suppose if you ask people if they want to be conquered you shouldn't be surprised if they say no.

Having subjugated the enemy, Alexander is truly great when it comes to integrating the conquered people into his empire, but it just leaves me with a feeling that there has to be a better way than killing masses of people to get what you want.

It seemed on reflection that what I needed was another mentor who would balance out Alexander, again I wondered what sort of person.

Mentor number two had to share big ideas so that the good points of mentor number one would not be diluted. A world figure who was respected for achieving big things yet who had humility so that when I got into my arrogant mode he would simply point out that other people had a view and that maybe I should consider a path which would have no bodies strewn along it.

In the 1960s I was sales director and trainer of a direct sell life insurance brokerage. We were all young, making lots of cash and very 'into' sales techniques. Some people would say that these techniques were manipulative and to a degree they were. As sales trainer I justified teaching and practising these techniques as I firmly believed that people need all the life insurance they can afford. Believe me, when you have seen the financial problems lifted from a young widow, it is easy to justify using emotive closing words to convince a reluctant husband that he should sign on the dotted line.

So we had an ever growing sales force making ever increasing pay cheques, driving bigger and more luxurious cars, having better holidays and going to more and wilder parties as was the way of that decade.

Along with this package came an insidious arrogance for those earning less and for those who didn't seem to want the same sort of fun or lifestyle.

In retrospect we were very unkind to some people who did not deserve our scorn and our score for consideration of others must have been at the lower end of the scale.

Of course most of us grew out of this state and learned some tolerance and possibly a little humility.

On a personal note I certainly see no point in making enemies and believe that great things can be achieved by co-operation.

My self audit showed that I did not like making enemies and Alexander's view was that enemies were OK as long as you beat the hell out of them. Arrogant or what? He also laughed at my tendency to ignore a fight and to attempt to be friends with every one.

Mentor number two would be a man of humility who achieved his aims by peaceful means and would counterbalance Alexander in the areas I felt were needed.

A man of soul.

Now that rang a bell.

MOHANDAS KARAMCHAND (MAHATMA) GANDHI
1869–1948

He was born on October 2nd 1869, in Porbanar, the capital of the small principality of Gujarat, Western India.

He was not an empire builder but took back for his people a large chunk of the British Empire. He became not only the pre-eminent leader of Indian Nationalism, but also the non-violent freedom fighter who was most influential in gaining Home Rule for India.

Any one who has seen the great film of his life can not fail to be moved by the scene where the Indians offered themselves up to receive a blow on the head from the British soldiers. They came rank after rank to demonstrate that they had a point and that whatever force was offered against them they would not be moved.

Karamchand, Gandhi's father, was a chief minister of Porbandar and although he had little formal education, he did have a certain political ability to move among the princes, their long-suffering subjects and the headstrong British political officers then in power.

Putibai, his mother, was completely absorbed in religion and divided her time between her home and the Temple. Gandhi therefore grew up in a home steeped in Vaisnavism, the worship of the Hindu god Vishnu with more than a hint of Jainism, a morally vigorous Indian religion whose chief tenets are non-violence and the belief that everything in the Universe is eternal.

He took for granted the principle of 'ahimsa', the non-injury of all living things, vegetarianism, fasting for self-purification and mutual tolerance between the various creeds and sects.

An excellent example of Gandhi's positive mental attitude, wisdom and philosophy that developed from these teachings came later in life. During a particularly vicious confrontation between Moslem Pakistan and Hindu India, he was approached by a distraught Hindu whose son had been killed by Moslems. In revenge, he himself had killed a Moslem child and came to Gandhi in despair, asking what he should do.

After due consideration, Gandhi said: "Go forth and find a Moslem child who has been orphaned by the riots. Take that Moslem child into your Hindu home and raise him as your own son, but, *as a Moslem.*"

Like many children of his time he was married at the tender age of thirteen thus losing a whole year of schooling but despite that he was still able to matriculate at the University of Bombay.

He went on to finish his education at the London University in England where, strangely, he was to first encounter what later became his very own 'spiritual dictionary'. It was the Bhagavadgita, the most popular expression of Hinduism in the form of a philosophical poem, which he read for the very first time in the English translation by Sir Edwin Arnold.

It was to become the most significant single influence in his life.

With his education complete, he returned to India to practice Law and developed a £5000 a year practice, which was a large sum of money at that time. No sooner had he achieved this than he gave it all up to go to Africa, to serve for just £1 a week for the next twenty-one years, opposing that country's discrimination against Indians.

Serving that cause with such a long-term commitment turned out to be an excellent apprenticeship in leadership that was to prove invaluable on his return to India in 1914.

Now with some years of non-violent campaigning experience behind him, he took up the cause of the 'Swaraj', or Home Rule Movement and in due course became the leader of the Congress organisation.

From 1920 onwards, he organised campaigns of non-violent civil disobedience and in 1930 lead a 200 mile march to the sea to collect salt in a symbolic protest against the government monopoly of that substance.

This strange sign of protest was to be the beginning of a major revolution for which Gandhi was blamed, arrested and jailed for his part in the action.

Although he was in and out of jail for much of the late 30's and early 40's, he never lost sight of his goals. He remained focused and despite long periods of imprisonment and self-induced fasting, he always emerged from jail fitter and stronger than when he went in.

Released in 1944, he negotiated the new constitutional structure with the British. 1947 was his finest hour and greatest triumph, the British decision to grant Independence. This he described politely as "The noblest act of the British Nation."

His final months were marred by continued strife between Moslem Pakistani and Hindu Indian factions who it would seem had not learned the lesson he taught. On 30th January 1948, he was assassinated by a Hindu fanatic.

However, the goal that he had held dear and fought for continuously over a full thirty-three years had become reality.

Gandhi has been venerated as a great moral and spiritual teacher, a reformer who sought to free India of its caste system and the patriot that gave the Home Rule Movement in India its moral force.

Through Faith alone, Mahatma Gandhi achieved his goals. He did it without resorting to violence. He did it without retaliating in kind. He did it without arrogance and with humility.

He was able to transplant that Faith into the minds of over 200,000,000 people !

He accomplished this astounding feat of influencing 200,000,000 minds to coalesce and move as a single mind.

Gandhi's was a well-lived and truly inspirational life and one that we can all take lessons from. He made himself one of the greatest benefactors of all time by the simple process of serving his countrymen without limit and without thought of financial reward.

He drew several hundred million of his Indian countrymen to him of their own free will, and his reward - the independence of his nation - was a reward greater than most of us ever dream of achieving

Although not arrogant, one of my favourite quotes of his is when asked what he thought of Western civilisation: he answered, "I think it would be a good idea".

Alexander would never have said it.

So I had my mentor number two.

Gandhi was not named Mahatma at birth but gained the name later in life.

It Means "Great Soul".

Something to do now

Think of a hero who has gentleness, faith and humanity but a firm underlying strength.

CHAPTER 6
Some Rules

When you have two strong characters advising you they do not always see eye to eye. Alexander turns out to be very headstrong and full of energy and ready to charge into anything, whereas Gandhi while quite willing to back me on any worthwhile project exercises a lot more caution. It is probably the lawyer in him.

Wouldn't it be great to have someone who could act as mentor number three who could maybe act as some sort of interface and put some structure into my collection of mentors; or my board of directors, as I am thinking of them?

What sort of person would fit the bill and help counter some more of my failings and develop my strengths?

It would be nice to have someone who was alive so that they could give some practical advice on how to apply whatever the other two came up with.

Perhaps someone with commercial experience. Someone who was doing what I was now doing and somebody who could perhaps supply some ground rules for dealing with the 21st Century.

I think every one likes ground rules. I enjoyed maths and physics at school because we learned of rules which govern much of the way the world and the universe works. It must have been a marvellous time to have been alive at the same time of Newton and his colleagues and to have been involved with discovery of so many basic laws.

Newton was certainly not alive and he didn't exactly fill the position I was looking for to fill my number three position.

Although I am not highly religious I like a lot of what Saint Paul stood for.

He is credited with first voicing the Golden Rule which now days we voice as "What goes round comes round". Gandhi would accept him on the board because the original Golden Rule emphasised the need to treat others in the same way that we would like to be treated ourselves. But again, he was not a current person.

I trawled my bookshelves for inspiration and many candidates offered themselves. I have the biographies and works of many inspirational people. What I wanted was a particular type of person who would balance the team recruited so far. Someone with a new message but who would appeal to the others in my mentor team.

Who was alive who had given me some rules of operation which were relevant to the modern world? They didn't even have to be his rules as long as he knew them and could explain why they were important and why they worked.

I examined some of my operating rules and remembered where I had got them from.

BRIAN TRACY

Brian Tracy has had more than one successful career. From sales and marketing, through investments, importation and distribution, management to becoming Chairman of Brian Tracy International he has achieved his goals.

He addresses thousands of men and women each year, including heads of industry and commerce, on the subject of leadership. He is the author of several books and audio programmes on such subjects as self esteem and success psychology.

His quiet style and logical approach seemed to me just what was needed to create some structure to my mentor list. I could picture him in session with the rest of the mentors telling us "How to take the chance out of becoming a success". In his programme of the same name he explains the following rules or Laws:

Action and Reaction, Sowing and Reaping, Averages, Attraction, Belief, Expectations, Subconscious Activity, Correspondence, Mental Equivalence, Responsibility, Serendipity, Synchronicity, Control, Purpose, Accident, Clarity, Desire, Accelerating Acceleration, 80/20, Concentration and about 40 other Laws including the most important Law of Abundance.

I particularly like the law of 80/20 which seems to apply to everything. In any organisation 20% of people do the work while 80% watch on. Any project seems to get nowhere for 80% of the time and then big results come in the last 20% and you can no doubt find many examples of this Law in your own life.

The Law of Abundance. Once discovered banishes greed forever. It is truly amazing that when you study this Law and tie it in to the Laws of Serendipity and Synchronicity, every action turns up the resources you need for any project.

The whole point is that over the years successful people have learned that certain actions get them what they want and that a different set of actions gets the reverse. The codification of these actions become the Laws of Success and to achieve success the Laws need to be obeyed. Even if the Laws can not be explained by science or logic they still need to be followed if the result of so doing is the achievement of the desired goal.

"What goes round comes round" is a Law which springs to mind as an example of this. Often the results of doing a favour or even a disservice to someone are not manifest immediately but rest assured you will get the just results and rewards of your actions sooner or later.

For some reason it gave me a great feeling of security to know that Brian was on my team. Perhaps it was that as someone said "Life is a Game" and any game has to have a set of rules so the players know what they are allowed to do and what the penalties are for breaking those rules.

As a rugby player we did not have rules but a set of Laws. These Laws governed my sporting life for nearly fifty years and became a pedestal on which much of my view of life was based.

The fair play concept, for instance, is Rugby through and through.

The other Law which influenced me gave rise to the inclusion of yet another mentor introduced in the next chapter but one…

Something to do now

Think of a hero who has a good set of rules to go by.

CHAPTER 7
Humanity

Without being morbid I would like you to consider your tombstone.

It will have two dates on it with a line in between.

The dates are not important; it is the line which is your life.

Your life and what you make of it is, in the main, to be decided by you.

You will have your successes and your failures. You will have your triumphs and disasters.

Most people like to forget their failures and disasters and remember their successes and triumphs.

Two of the greatest attributes and which all true heroes have are humility and humanity. Humility and humanity come from realising that you are human with human frailties. To realise that your time is limited and that immortality is reserved for the gods is a great step towards this.

The great thing about Super Heroes, particularly in the sporting world, is the gracious acceptance of both winning and losing. This takes nothing away from their competitiveness.

A becoming modesty when on the rostrum or when interviewed by the media creates fans who will follow the star for their personality as well as their achievements.

When we gain success we can be proud of ourselves. We can bask in any glory that is being handed out. We should enjoy the fruits of our labours, after all, that is why we laboured.

There is an old show business adage. "Be nice to the people you meet on the way up. You will meet them again on the way down".

That is good advice. Ignore it at your peril and you will be in danger of becoming arrogant.

I am not proud of the way I dealt with some people in the past through having a misguided streak of arrogance. It is one thing to be confident of one's abilities and quite another to be big headed and arrogant.

Most people like to see arrogant people being taken down a peg or two yet those same people love to see a humble person succeed and continue to succeed. They think more of them because of their humility.

The point is that people with humanity don't think less of themselves, they think of themselves less.

I knew that my new team of advisors would give me great success and that I would have to guard against my old arrogant streak resurfacing so who could I get to join the team who would keep my feet on the ground?

I wanted no negative influence and I did not want to dilute the aggressiveness of Alexander The Great and I did not want to duplicate Gandhi. Brian Tracy, I know would welcome someone on the team who would be an example of the rules in operation. The ideal person would be someone who was a great military leader but also who had a philosophy which recognised the essential temporary nature of our time on this planet. A visit to my bookshelf and the cinema provided the answer.

MARCUS AURELIUS Emperor of Rome 161–180 AD

If you have seen the epic film Gladiator it is unlikely you will forget the opening sequence.

In the battle the Romans dealt with their enemies in ruthless fashion. The war machine that was the Roman army deployed their troops and their fire hurling ballistas with frightening efficiency and destroyed the opposing forces with what may have been seen as cool indifference.

The leader of the Roman forces was Marcus Aurelius, Emperor of Rome from AD161 to his death in AD181.

It may be hard to imagine that such a man could be classified as one who had the quality of humanity.

During his time as Emperor he witnessed the gradual decline of the Roman Empire. He saw its borders shrink and famines and plagues strike the population.

He began to study the Stoic philosophy. While he was in the area of the Danube he began to record his thoughts now famously known as his Meditations.

These thoughts show a great insight into the transitory nature of human material gains. Without dwelling on death there are many thoughts which make the reader realise that one day there is an end for every one as far as living on this earth goes. Further, that the achievements of life may well ultimately count for nothing.

Having said that there are more than enough snippets of his thoughts to provide pragmatic guidance in building a meaningful life while keeping ones feet firmly on the ground.

For example I like the encouraging thought *"Because a thing is difficult for you, do not suppose it to be beyond mortal power. On the contrary, if anything is possible and proper for a man to do, assume that it must fall within your own capacity"*.

"Waste not time arguing what a good man should be. Be one.", is practical.

"To live each day as though one's last, never flustered, never apathetic, never attitudinising – here is perfection of character." is simply just great advice.

When you read some of his longer thoughts where he asks you to consider the thought that after you have gone you will be remembered in the thoughts of people until they too are gone, a feeling of what it means to be human sweeps over you.

At this point some thought as to what life is really about takes place.

Yes Marcus needs to be on the team to make sure that at all times I am living in the real world. Some of his meditations will serve to back up the rules Brian Tracy has contributed.

Just one thought. Is Marcus a little on the depressing side sometimes?

Something to do now

Think of a hero who will remind you to keep a sense of perspective and remind you that you are a mortal human being.

CHAPTER 8
Words

I mentioned in Chapter 6 that there was another Law worth looking at.

There are no ladies on my panel of advisers but that is not to say that there is no influence from them. I most certainly recognise the vast influence of my wife and life partner Bren and of course that of my mother.

I no doubt inherited my love of words in all forms and in the written form in particular from my mother. My father was pedantic about the correct use of words and it was a rare occasion to hear him utter a swear word but it was my mother who taught me to read at a very early age and who showed me how to learn from books.

I was guided by her choice of reading material which, it must be said, gave me some very coloured views as to religion, race and The Great British Empire. Being a second world war baby and having my formative years in post war Britain many of my heroes were Battle of Britain pilots and their counterparts in Bomber Command, The Navy and The Army.

As I read more I saw that that these valiant heroes were merely carrying the baton of such early defenders of British Freedom such as Wellington, Drake, General Gordon, Nelson and Baden Powell. These were, it seemed to me, extensions of the Roman and Greek heroes who were acceptable due to their antiquity.

I became extremely confused by my mothers statements regarding black people, Germans, Arabs and her generalisations which were contradicted by her extreme kindness and generosity to any one in need of help and assistance. She professed to have been a member of Oswald Mosely's Black Shirts yet she had several Jewish Friends whom she clearly liked immensely and would have given her last penny to had they needed it.

Her views on Germany as the enemy (reinforced by my observation of the bomb damage in Manchester) were strangely at odds with her insistence that we entertain German Prisoners of War on parole in the Pre-fab in which we lived in that city during the early 1940s.

My mothers great prejudices made me have a very black and white prejudicial attitude to many things yet her behaviour created doubts in my mind as to the foundations of these views. Later in Life I was able to sort out my own views but at that time I needed a code to help me.

My mother was forever quoting the words of a certain poem to me and from time to time the words of another verse by the same author were also meaningful to me.

For most of my life I now recognise that I have made so many conscious and sub conscious decisions based on these two works that the author must be on the team. Not only will his presence remind me of the importance of words but also that so much wisdom can be contained in verse.

RUDYARD KIPLING 1865–1936

The first of his poems I recall being told is the classic **IF** and the second is The Law Of The Jungle.

I was speaking to a friend some time ago who at 55 had just been declared bankrupt. Someone had given him a copy of IF and it was the first time he had seen it. His spirits were raised and he realised that he could start again.

Rudyard Kipling was born in Bombay in 1865, the son of talented and artistic parents.

When he was twelve he was sent to school at the United Services College at Westward Ho!

The headmaster who was a friend of his father and uncles nurtured his latent literary ability. His poor eye sight proved a handicap in games but he blossomed in other areas.

In 1882 aged 16 he returned to Lahore to work on the Civil and Military Gazette and in his spare time he wrote many short stories and poems. When these were collected and published as books he started to become famous. He returned to England in 1889 and was married in 1892.

After a world trip he returned to Vermont with his American bride with the intention of settling there. He wrote the Jungle Books and became a father twice but a quarrel with his brother in law made him return to England in 1896 and took up residence in Sussex and became a father again.

By the turn of the century Kipling had come to be regarded as the People's Laureate and the poet of the British Empire.

He was very productive and I find his works so varied.

If I were to have a top ten of favourite poems I am sure he would contribute four or five.

Not only have such poems as If, Gunga Din and The Law of the Jungle contributed to my basic philosophy but others such as The Roman Centurion's Song, The Way Through The Woods and The Land I find moving and spiritual.

Words to me are a concrete expression of thoughts and I am pleased to have such a master on the team.

Something to do now

Choose a literary person to join your team.

Find a writer who has expressed the things you believe in.

Find a writer who has the ability through his or her work to move you emotionally.

CHAPTER 9
Luck

Is there such a thing as luck and if so how can we access it?

If there is such a thing as luck are there two types, bad and good luck?

If luck exists how come some people seem to get more than their fair share?

I am pretty certain I will never win the football pools or the lottery. Is that because I do not consider myself lucky? No, not at all. It is because I never buy a ticket or fill in a pools coupon.

I know that if you don't play the game you have no chance of winning but I prefer better odds and a little more control over the outcome.

Some people say that luck is being in the right place at the right time.

There is no doubt that circumstances outside our control have bearing on our lives but how we deal with them can have a greater effect.

Was there a reason why so called lucky people were in the right place at the right time? Were they lucky or were they actually in the game when their number was called?

There is the much posed question; "do we make our own luck?". If we do, do we make our own bad luck and our own good luck?

Are we in control or are our lives in the lap of the gods?

Let us take the pendulum swing view.

We are either in control or we are not. Either our every move is predetermined by an external force or it is not.

If the latter is true why bother about any thing. Life is already written out for us, our destiny is mapped and there is nothing we can do about it.

If on the other hand we can influence our lives and our achievements should we not choose what we want and maximise every opportunity to get it?

If we did the first we would be relying on luck. If we did the second we would be making our own luck.

Let us not confuse luck with chance.

Most situations have a number of possible outcomes. Some have only two. Some have millions.

The decision to jump over the edge of a high cliff without a parachute has two possible outcomes with one more likely than the other.

The decision to buy a lottery ticket has two outcomes but the probability of the good result happening has odds running into millions.

In either case a decision can be made. In neither case can the result be absolutely guaranteed and "luck" comes into play.

The point is that you do not have to place yourself in either situation; this is true of many good and bad luck situations. You have an incredible amount of control over how you deal with the twists and turns of life and more importantly over those actual twists and turns.

It may be "bad luck" to get caught for speeding on a road where you have exceeded the limit every day for the last six years. Whose decision was it that you drove at that speed?

It may be good luck that you meet someone at a party who is looking for a service you supply. Who made the decision to go to the party?

Luck

It may be "good luck" that a friend calls you to tell you about a rare item for your collection that is available at a good price. Whose decision was it to make your friend aware that you were in the market for such an item?

We talk elsewhere of the power of the sub conscious and the power of visions. Could this explain why some people seem to get all the luck while others get none?

There is a power of expectation. Expect a good outcome and it happens more often than not and the reverse is also true.

I believe the simple explanation that every event has the seeds of "luck" within it. If you perceive the good that is what will be manifested by your exploitation of the circumstances. If you perceive the bad then that is what you will get because that is all you can see.

Two thousand five hundred years ago the world believed that the Gods controlled our feeble lives. Sacrifices had to be made to appease these immortal beings otherwise they would wreak havoc and disaster upon us.

Even though sacrifices were made often bad results occurred. The Gods were displeased.

About this time in Ancient Greece philosophers were beginning to realise that this was not the case. What if there were such a thing as cause and effect?

What if we had a degree of control over our lives which was nothing to do with celestial beings whose mere whim decided what became of us?

Later on in the time of Newton science advanced and gave us explanations for much of the way the world operates. There had to be a reason why things happened in the way they did. Cause and effect again.

It is to the Ancient Greeks however that I look for someone to join the team who will remind me that the outcome of my life depends mainly on me and how I deal with the cards I am dealt and that to a certain extent I can affect the deal.

ARISTOTLE 384–322 BC

Aristotle was born in Macedonia, the son of Nicomachus, personal physician to the King.

At the age of 17 Aristotle left Stagira to attend school in Athens. He attended the Academy founded by Plato and set up to provide a continual educational experience. There he stayed for nearly twenty years until Plato died in 347.

Aristotle was seen as a brilliant although independent student and he had hoped to succeed Plato as director of the Academy but Speusippus, a nephew of Plato, was chosen as the heir to Plato. In addition, as Aristotle was not an Athenian by birth he was subject to the anti-Macedonian feelings rife at that time.

He therefore left Athens in 347 and travelled the Greek Islands and in Asia Minor until 343.

It was in 343 that Aristotle accepted an invitation from Phillip, King of Macedonia, to become the tutor of his son – no less than Alexander The Great.

It is reported that there was great interaction between the two. Aristotle wanted to retain Greek culture and Alexander wanted to amalgamate the Greek culture with non-Greek; the better to govern the outlying provinces.

In 335 Aristotle had returned to Athens where he lectured at the Lyceum for 12 years. Here his works covered areas of thought from ethics to politics, from metaphysics through logic to science.

He developed a non Platonic theory which rivalled that of his tutor for the next 2000 years.

When Alexander died in 323 the old anti Macedonian faction gained strength and Aristotle retired to Chalices where he died in 322 aged 63.

His thoughts have been an inspiration to people who like to challenge the accepted knowledge of the day and his logic made it possible to advance science. People no longer believed that their fate was in the lap of the gods and I like to think that perhaps he was the first person to utter the words "If it is to be it is up to me".

Something to do now

Choose a hero who will remind you that what you get is what you deserve through the actions you take.

CHAPTER 10
Leadership

All the members of my advisory team are leaders in some way or other.

Some are military leaders others leaders in their chosen field.

I admire the qualities of a leader and know that every one needs to be the leader of their own life if they are to get what they want.

If you are not a leader then you are a follower and if you are following are you necessarily being led in the direction you want to go?

When I talk about self leadership I am not suggesting that you will have a host of people behind you whose ultimate fate rests on you. I simply mean that to commit to a course of action which is designed to lead you to a predetermined destination will require a degree of vision and persistence. It will require you to decide on your values and to stick with them in the face of adversity.

If you are clear as to what you want to achieve and are sure that it is a meaningful and worthwhile goal you will need a certain inner strength to maintain your efforts when things go wrong and when other people try to divert you.

You may in some situations need to make a sacrifice of some kind for the greater good, as you see it.

Only leadership skills will take you through these times.

Leaders who do not have a clear vision are easily swayed to take the easy route. This could be simply because the easy route may look more attractive in the short term or because they lack the courage to make an unpopular decision.

Either way are these people demonstrating true leadership?

Imagine that you have a very clear picture of what you want out of life. See yourself pursuing this picture with all the energy and enthusiasm you can muster until you reach it. You see yourself meeting all the obstacles and beating them no matter what the odds.

Even if no one else is involved you will have demonstrated the actions of a leader.

Now imagine yourself with the same picture but your goals change every day.

Sometimes you change them because you think you have a better vision or because someone has told you that your original picture was a non starter. Some times you go for a different goal because the difficulties you have encountered seem insurmountable.

You are demonstrating the characteristics of a follower. You will not finish up with what you want but with what others want, if anything at all.

So is it a tall order to be a leader?

To be a great leader the answer is yes. To be a self leader the answer is not such a big yes.

Both situations demand the same characteristics and actions but to a differing degree.

The great leader has bigger and more far reaching decisions to make. Far bigger sacrifices perhaps involving life or death decisions.

Your decisions may not have such heavy ramifications as those of an international leader but they will have a very great effect on your own life and on the lives of the people with whom you are involved.

If you are to lead yourself to the destination of your life time achievements you will need to cultivate and develop some skills and attitudes you may not have developed so far.

Without vision, where are you going?

Without courage how will you meet the challenges you will meet?

Without persistence how will you stick to your path?

Without compassion how will you have others involved of their own free will?

Without passion how will you communicate your vision to others and yourself?

Without persistence how will you keep up the work until you arrive?

Without a sense of destiny how will you be sure that your vision is for you?

If you are not your own leader who will you follow?

Who is a leader you admire who you would follow if your goals were the same? Who would you choose? Who has the qualities you would like?

Alexander the Great is a fine leader and is on my team for his many leadership attributes and his ambition but the person who is on the team for his leadership skills had his weaknesses, but none in the area of leadership in my opinion.

WINSTON SPENCER CHURCHILL

As a child of World War II Churchill is a part of my early memories.

He was in the conversation of my parents and was ever present on the radio and even after the war was a constant feature in news reels.

With the post hostilities reviews there was much footage of him and there was an increasing amount of material reviewing his earlier life. Books were written about him. He was involved in politics until very late in life. A film was made of his early life and he was the first commoner to appear on a British postage stamp.

His bulldog profile with trademark cigar was instantly recognisable as was his voice.

There were many heroes in the war but it was Churchill who represented and led them. It was he who acknowledged their achievements and he who was responsible for planning and co-ordinating those efforts and sacrifices.

He knew that he would be sending men and women to their deaths. He new that the bombs and rockets of the German forces would fall on Britain but he was firm and resolute in leading the country to his vision of freedom.

His oratory skills and his talent for using the right words at the right time enabled him to communicate with the masses in a way which inspired lesser people to big achievements.

His famous speeches created and transmitted his vision of a free United Kingdom and Empire not only to it's members but also to its enemies. His call for self sacrifice and steadfastness of purpose in the face of whatever adversity was to come, stiffened the resolve of everyone in Britain and must have cast doubts into the minds of our enemies.

His vast experience gained in the Boer War and World War I steeled him for the ruthless decisions he had to make if Britain was not to succumb to the opposing forces.

His life, which contained many setbacks, gave him the knowledge that persistence would overcome all obstacles given time.

Time was valuable. Churchill was not a young man as leader of a war torn country and the very resources of the country were finite and running low.

Recognising the value of time he would issue instructions with the prominent comment **"Action this day"**.

When I am building a project it is great to have the team all contributing in their own ways with their individual valued input.

However, it is to Churchill I have to answer if I do not take the action I need to fulfil the goal.

He tells me to get started and it is he who will stop me from quitting on a project.

I can still hear his voice telling the population and perhaps, more importantly, Adolf Hitler "We will never, never, never, never give in".

Something to do now

Choose a hero you admire who will keep you on your toes and who you regard as a great leader.

CHAPTER 11
Humour

Life, regardless of the tightest planning rarely unfolds exactly as one would hope.

Regardless of what outside forces make happen to you there is one vital component of attitude which will help you overcome those adverse events and which will help you through the difficult times.

It is of course a sense of humour.

I have seen, countless times, two people placed in the same situation which represents some form of setback and observed the different ways that the two people have dealt with it.

The first may set about bemoaning their bad luck and imagining that things will go from bad to worse while the other adopts a wry smile, makes some sort of joke and starts to convert the situation to one of benefit.

I am not sure from where we derive our sense of humour or if there is any scientific basis for it.

I do know that without a sense of humour life would be more difficult than it is.

It seems to me that there is perhaps no intrinsic humour in many a situation but that it is possible to perceive humour.

It is said that beauty is in the eye of the beholder and so perhaps humour is in the mind of the beholder.

I have certainly been on the receiving end of some misfortune which other people have said would floor them and yet I have come out laughing.

I firmly believe that a sense of humour enables one to see the advantages of a misfortune and to diminish the effects it may otherwise have.

So onto the team must be recruited someone who has the ability to see the funny side and will help stop me crying into my beer if I have a setback.

This person must have a view point which is unlike most other peoples' view of life as I want a reminder that the humour I seek can be drawn from the darkest situation.

It is strange how many of our top comedians are sad and depressed people deep down. I think of Tony Hancock as an example of someone who made me laugh, yet was so depressed that he died before his time, from taking an overdose.

I want someone who doesn't just have a store of funny stories and jokes but someone with an almost surreal way of looking at a situation. An irreverent attitude to authority would be great as I tend to have too much respect for the establishment which can be stifling.

A breath of wicked humorous input would be great.

For me there is only one candidate.

SPIKE MILLIGAN

Spike Milligan owes me. Were it not for him I may have had a university education and who knows what success in business, commerce or the forces.

In the years prior to my GCE examinations I was an avid fan of "The Highly Esteemed Goon Show".

Instead of concentrating on my home work I would sit, ears glued, to our radio listening to every word of this show.

At the time it was ground breaking humour which not all the grown ups appreciated and the BBC were a little hesitant to air at the start.

The combination of silly voices, strange sound effects and manic plots with crazy catch phrases became an essential part of any schoolboy's life.

Such was the influence of this innovative show that Monty Python et al. will acknowledge where their basic style has its origins.

Even today I cannot hear a repeat, even though I know what is coming, without dissolving into helpless laughter.

The Goons chemistry relied not only on Spike but also Peter Sellars and Harry Secombe but it was Spike who wrote the scripts.

He wrote 26 scripts a year from 1951 to 1960. He had a dozen nervous breakdowns and became a nation wide famous manic depressive.

It is not just for his humour I have him on the team. I firmly believe that his type of humour contains the same trait which enables new business opportunities to be seen where they may otherwise be invisible.

There is no denying that any mind which sees a man who has lost his dog placing a newspaper advertisement saying "Here boy!" has a different view.

The celebrated Min and Henry sequence in the Goons always had a strange sense of logic about it.

"What's the weather like Min?" asks Henry.

"I don't know Henry, I can't see through the snow."

If you can appreciate that you are bound to see a way through or around some obstruction in life. It just happens.

Winston Churchill was once on a tour of inspection when Spike was in the army.

"And what do you do?", asked the great man.

"I do my best, sir". What courage.

Prince Charles is a fellow devotee and he was no doubt hurt when Spike described him as "a little grovelling bastard".

Spike sent a telegram saying "I suppose a knighthood is out of the question now?", and was soon back in favour. In fact he was awarded an honorary knighthood some time later.

So many people have seen Spike, as a guest, on some TV show create absolute havoc as his brand of humour goes wild, that you may wonder what I am doing with a manic depressive loose cannon on my team.

Well it is a matter of balance and I just love the way that Spike acts as a catalyst to the other members.

Something to do now

Choose a hero who has a sense of humour which appeals to you and which has that twisted element which encourages you to see things in a different way to normal.

CHAPTER 12
Balance

Enthusiasm is one of the greatest attributes in any persons character.

It is that infectious energy for a project which is so contagious that every one involved catches it and in so doing contributes their own energies.

Lack of enthusiasm is also contagious and I have seen many a person spoil a worthwhile enterprise through their pessimistic outlook killing the project before it even gets on the drawing board.

Without enthusiasm it is unlikely that anything will be achieved and if you possess it you indeed have a head start over the rest of the world.

I have many positive people on my team and in general they ask the question "Why not?" as opposed to putting forward the negative view.

Now, as a person full of enthusiasm and with a high degree of optimism it is not unknown for me to have set out on a project without full consideration of all possible outcomes and with little planning.

To be fair this has helped me seize passing opportunities which may have been lost at a later date. It has also landed me in trouble more than once.

On balance things have worked out for the best but a little more circumspection at the right time would have been even more beneficial.

'On balance'. That is what is now required in my team. A balancing force.

I was once asked if I was efficient by someone who wanted to know if I was effective and we had quite a debate over the meaning of the two words.

We decided that it was possible to be effective in that the goal was reached but that it was not necessarily achieved in an efficient manner. For example if too many resources were used the job may well be completed but the cost would rise.

I read that most entrepreneurs tend to ignore the cost in chasing their goals; the attainment of the objective being the focus.

This may be all very well where resources are plentiful but what about where they are precious?

You may have a burning ambition to become a millionaire. You may be in the peak of health and have the support of your loving family.

How would you feel if your focus on working hard were to damage your health? If you lost your family due to an ever increasing need to be involved with your business, would it all have been worth it?

Surely the answer must be no. Would it not be better to achieve your goal, maintain your health, have a lifestyle which enabled you to devote time to your friends and family and have a life where you are committing your time to what is important, in the right proportions?

I have seen too many people burn themselves out sometimes before they enjoy the fruits of their labours and sometimes they have died exhausted just as they achieved their aim.

I have seen salesmen hit their targets at the cost of their marriage.

There has to be a better way.

With my team assembled and being ready to go I need an additional member whose role it will be to ensure that balance which will get me effective **and** efficient results.

I want the enthusiasm channelled so that all areas of my life receive their due proportion of my efforts.

Who is a world famous figure who knows how to achieve this?

I am fortunate to meet regularly with Britain's top business and personal development coaches. There is one name which never fails to come up in conversation at our meetings.

He must be on the team.

STEPHEN R COVEY

The Seven Habits of Highly Effective People by Stephen Covey (Simon & Schuster) has sold over 10 Million copies world wide and it is no wonder to me.

His book presents an all encompassing method based on a principle -centred approach for the resolution of personal and professional problems.

His values of fairness, honesty, integrity and human dignity are those to which we should all aspire. I certainly identified with his views and took the opportunity to utilise some of his code in formulating and defining my own values.

In a later chapter I record thirty principles by which I try and live and a few of these came into being after reading Stephen's book.

Brian Tracy, whom you met in an earlier chapter says of Stephen, *"Stephen R Covey is an American Socrates, opening your mind to the "permanent things" – values, family relationships, communicating."*

Some of his fundamentals are so basic yet so important.

He counsels us to understand other people before we seek to be understood. He urges us to make every transaction win/win.

He shows us how to achieve that essential balance by learning how to give and to receive.

One of his important principles is to make sure we recharge our batteries. This can only be done if balance is achieved.

The pay off in terms of efficiency can not be denied.

We all need enough sleep. We all need to keep our minds sharp. Only by stepping back from time to time and giving ourselves a "service" can we operate at peak efficiency.

In the book we are not only guided as to maintaining our bodily and mental well being but we are shown that relationships need to be nurtured if they are not to be one sided.

How true that is. If we let our consideration for others fall we may find that we have used up all our credit with people, having the result that we no longer have valuable and essential backing.

So with Stephen R Covey on the team I am sure that balance will be maintained.

I am not in the least concerned that my enthusiasm or sense of urgency will be diminished in the long term as overall efficiency will enable more to be done in less time.

I am not worried that too much time will be spent on soul searching, as any dilemma is easily resolved by reference to the principles.

If balance is achieved there are fewer nasty surprises and more involvement with other like minded people.

You may be thinking that all this may sound a bit ephemeral and theoretic.

Keep in mind that the first of Stephen's 7 Habits is: **BE PROACTIVE**

Something to do now

Choose a model person who has values you can take as your own and who will advise you to keep that essential balance in your life.

CHAPTER 13
Doing it now

The team is almost complete. There is such a wealth of talent, experience, knowledge and wisdom. I have leaders and men of words. I have examples of naked ambition and of humility and humanity. I have humour and logic. I have spontaneous input and balance in outlook and destination. So what is lacking?

What is lacking in most of us; the final spark that makes us get up off the couch in front of the television and get on with the job; that energy which makes us do just that little bit extra to make the difference?

And that difference doesn't have to be huge. Take a look at the Downhill Men's Ski Championship and see the top five separated by hundredths of a second. Watch Formula one Grand Prix racing and see the second car come in half a second after the leader and that after maybe seventy laps at top speed.

So the difference between first and second is marginal but the difference between the competitors and the spectators is vast.

The question is are you to be a spectator or a competitor? That was my question.

You have probably gathered I like to do a fair bit of planning before I act, although I have been known to plunge headlong into ventures and projects with absolutely no preparation.

The secret is as always to strike the balance. What the team needs is someone who is living proof of the cliché "Massive Action equals Massive Results".

Who do I know who works harder than I ever will. Who is a shining example of someone who works hard and plays hard. Who do I know who I could compare my efforts and his efforts and his results with my results and say to myself, "Boy, you had better try a bit harder".

A few years ago I became involved in a business which has several such people and it has been a privilege to work with them and to be associated with them. I have learned from their example and although my ambitions do not lie in exactly the same area as do theirs they have given freely of their time. Cliff Walker, Geoff Liberman, Jeremy Taylor, Ray Cranston, Michael Heppell and Paul Fitzgerald are just six names and there is more about our business in Chapter 29.

These people put in many hours a week developing not only their own businesses but those of others in the organisation and I have the uttermost respect for them and their colleagues who are tracing if not trampling the same path.

As I say in Chapter 29, it is a business which every ambitious person interested in personal development, time and money freedom would do well to examine.

There is one other name who has been of a little more support and inspiration to me than Cliff and the others named above and that man has to be the final team member.

STEVE MITCHELL

I first met Steve Mitchell when I attended a business presentation in early 1999. I had just joined the business and Steve had joined it some eight months earlier. Steve was hosting the meeting and he had put together a presentation followed by a training.

The atmosphere was electric with, it must be said, very loud music. There were probably eight hundred people in the room. Steve was buzzing around the stage coordinating a team of speakers who were given the limelight when they were on and I was struck by the way Steve edified them for their achievements.

Later on Steve told me of his philosophy that the best way to become a star is to be a starmaker. It is a philosophy I have adapted to good advantage and one which I heartily recommend.

Steve is a man of immense energy and he freely and generously gives of himself in supporting people in his team. What more could I ask for a member of my team.

During one of the times Steve has stayed at our house I quizzed Steve about the application of his philosophy. I also wished to support people who needed my support but was experiencing frustration that my efforts on their behalf were not being reciprocated.

Naturally Steve had been through this and counselled me on how to give people one hundred percent support as long as they were applying their efforts on a consistent basis. He taught me that not everyone has the same goals and that certainly my goals were not theirs. He demonstrated that there was no reason to mar a longstanding relationship just because a business colleague did not have the same energy, ambition and commitment as myself.

Steve has introduced me to an audience as the "A man who walks the talk". That description is much more befitting of him.

He has had his ups and downs in life. He built up a chain of Pizza outlets and lost the lot but did not let that stand in his way of recovery.

He has become an inspirational speaker and leader not only to the eight and a half thousand people in his new business but also to the rest of the people in the company of which Steve's business is a part. He has been rewarded by being promoted from a self employed independent consultant of the company to Field Sales Director which is true recognition for his tremendous efforts.

As well as working his socks off he enjoys breaks on the Ski slopes and has a penchant for seventies parties. He meets his goals: one of which was to take delivery of a brand new Porsche on his fortieth birthday. A long standing ambition.

OK Starmaker, you are the only member of the team I asked in the flesh, as it were, if you would join and you will never know how much it pleased me that you said yes.

Something to do now

Choose a live hero, someone who is a real example to you as regards "doing it". Who is it who shames you by his or her application to their goals and yet enjoys life to the full?

CHAPTER 14
Introducing DR SPACE™

So here I was with my team of mentors. Ten people who would serve as heroes, role models where I needed them to be, and who would act as guardians of my values when the advice they gave me as individuals needed modifying in some way. In the main they were selected for either a positive boost to my strengths and or coaches to help me with my weaknesses.

Alexander The Great	Naked Ambition
Gandhi	Faith & Humility
Brian Tracy	Universal Rules
Marcus Aurelius	Humanity
Rudyard Kipling	Words
Winston Churchill	Leadership
Aristotle	Responsibility
Spike Milligan	Humour
Stephen Covey	Balance & Efficiency
Steve Mitchell	Work rate, Enthusiasm & Energy

But would it be difficult dealing with ten people at once? Not at all. In some strange flash of inspiration, insight, maybe craziness, I saw an amalgamated personality I could deal with for the majority of the time and for some unknown reason he was called DR SPACE™.

DR SPACE™ would be my mentor. He would have all the good characteristics of my team of ten. He would be there for me at any time.

He was pretty well perfect because of his combined knowledge and skills.

As I started to work with DR SPACE™ I noticed that if there was a problem which needed a special kind of assistance then DR SPACE™ would seem to fade gently to be replaced by one of the ten component members whose particular talent was needed at this time.

Sometimes when the individual mentor gave advice which was a touch out of line with the overall game plan, instead of DR SPACE™ reforming, one of the other team members would manifest and often quite interesting discussions would take place before the issue was resolved.

You should hear Alexander The Great arguing a point with Winston Churchill after they have both been on the Brandy.

The point is that if you want to achieve things which have been achieved by other people you only have to do what they did. If there is something you wish to achieve which your heroes could have achieved you only have to do what they would have done.

Something to do now

Self Audit Exercise

My ten strengths are:

1. _____

2. _____

3. _____

4. _____

5. _____

6. _____

7. _____

8. _____

9. _____

10. _____

My ten weaknesses are:

1. _____

2. _____

3. _____

4. _____

5. _____

6. _____

7. _____

8. _____

9. _____

10. _____

Something else to do now

List your ten heroes together with the strength or weakness they will help you with.

My ten heroes who can help me are:	What they will help me with:
HERO	**Strength/weakness**

1. _____   _____

2. _____   _____

3. _____   _____

4. _____   _____

5. _____   _____

6. _____   _____

7. _____   _____

8. _____   _____

9. _____   _____

10. _____   _____

Congratulations! You have identified your perceived strengths and weaknesses.

You have identified your ten heroes who can help you.

You have your own personal DR SPACE™.

Although you don't know it you have much more than a team of mentors.

You have been introduced to DR SPACE™. Now meet

THE DR SPACE™ PROCESS

Having a team of mentors is one thing. Using them effectively is quite another.

What is required is a system.

McDonalds is a system. Any franchise is a system and you deviate from it at your peril.

How would it be if you had a system which you could apply to any situation to get the best out of it?

Imagine having a set of instructions which, provided you followed them, would lead you to achieving things you only dreamt of previously.

As I have said earlier, to achieve the success gained by others you only have to do the things they have done.

When you understand the process you will be able to start at once on building the future you want.

When you gain your first success, and it may be large or small, you will be able to teach the process to others and your success rate will multiply.

I have used the process to start projects which I have been delaying for ages. I have used it to finish projects lying on the shelf, half started. I have finalised new projects ahead of schedule.

I am in a better position to make and deliver bigger promises than before.

I get more work done in less time.

So can you.

The DR SPACE™ Process will assist you to work out what you want, when you want it and what you have to do to get it. It will help you stay on track and most importantly will enable you to enjoy the fruits of success.

There are seven steps to success.

They are:

Dream
Reason
Specify
Plan
Action
Commitment
Enjoyment

and we will examine them one by one.

CHAPTER 15
Dreams

It is a hot sunny day with a mild sea breeze. You are lying on the sun bed with your eyes closed.

You can hear the waves breaking on the shore just a few yards away. Beside you is your life partner.

The heat doesn't bother you because the breeze keeps the temperature down to a comfortable level and neither does the intense sun in the clear blue sky because you have blocker on and in any case at this time you are under the shade of a large beach umbrella.

The reason you guard against excess sun is because you take care of your body. You take care of your mind also and lying on the sand is a motivational personal development book. It may perhaps be the autobiography of a successful person whom you admire. You have just finished it.

As you drift in and out of a lazy sleep your peace is disturbed by the thought that maybe you haven't said or done some things in life that you always wanted.

As this thought grows and takes shape you seem to have an ever growing list of things that you wished you had done.

You turn and look at your life partner and wonder whether you could have done more, provided more.

You make a resolution. You will do more.

Your list grows more. You wonder whether you ought to stop adding things. Maybe the burden of such a task list is not possible.

Which of the things should you leave out?

Dreams

Where will the money come to pay for everything?

Where will you find the time to do what is necessary?

But you dream on.

For one thing it would be great to be able to lie here on the beach for more days than this short vacation. It would be great not to have to stay in the hotel but to buy the little place on the cliffs and maybe spend a couple of months every year at this your all time favourite place.

A thought springs to mind. Maybe you could buy the little place on the cliff and rent it out when you did not want it for your own occupation.

Another thought. Perhaps you could retire here or at least semi retire. Maybe get a part time job in the area or even start up a business. After all land is cheap, labour is cheap and people would flock to your business so that you could put in a trusted manager and you would only have to come in once a day to pick up the money to bank and once a week to pay the staff.

At this point you fall asleep again. You wake up because the sun has gone behind a cloud and you are not as warm as you were. You realise it is time to go back to the hotel for a shower before dinner. You realise also that tomorrow is the last full day of your holiday and you start to think about what is happening back at the office.

The dreams have floated away on the clouds which are drifting across the sun as the sea breeze stiffens up.

Your dreams may surface from time to time, maybe next week, as those little fluffy clouds gather mass and momentum and become part of a storm which gets you soaking wet back home.

They may not surface until next year when you come back for more sun, sand and relaxation.

But reappear they will for we always dream of what might be.

If we leave it too late we dream instead of what might have been.

Rudyard Kipling in "IF" instructs you to dream but not to make dreams your master.

But that is what most people do.

The dreams never come to realisation. They stay dreams.

As dreams written in cloud and borne on the wind they drift away, always out of reach.

So why don't we capture them? Why don't we turn them into reality? We don't we live our dreams?

I was told that everything happens twice. It happens first in the mind and second in reality.

What I believe happens is that as we lie on our personal beach our dreams happen in the mind but often before we can bring them to reality we substitute another dream. One that the good picture can't happen due to all the obstructions and constraints associated with realising the dream.

We dream that we can't do a thing rather than that we can. In so doing we let the first and nicer dream drift away, possibly for ever.

The answer is so simple and any one can do it.

Do not write your dreams on clouds, write them on paper.

Get your self an exercise book or a file and write them down before the sea breeze blows them away.

I have a book where I list everything I want to do or have. I am not greedy but as life gets better I think of more things so they get added.

I am not concerned at this stage as to how I am going to get them. I just want to make sure that they do not blow out of sight.

Every so often I take a look at the book and see if some of the things I want are more important to me than when I wrote them in. It is amazing how some things which "it would be nice to have" suddenly become possibilities.

Something to do now

Make sure you have a book or at least some paper to record your dreams.

Take some time out to have a dream session.

Do not put any limitations on what you think you would like. Remember this is a dream world and you can have anything you want.

If you wish you can be outrageous. In dream world there are no limits.

Ask you partner what his or her dreams are. Chances are that there will be many items on your list which you will both enjoy at a later date.

To emphasise this when I am dreaming guess where I dream.

That's right. In SPACE. The horizons are pretty broad up there and the planet looks very tiny so my dreams can be as large as I want them. A further benefit is that the gravity is less so my feet can easily leave the ground.

I know that soon I will need to land. I know that I will have to come back to reality just as our beach dreamers will return to work at the end of their vacation.

The difference is that we will have a book, a written record of those dreams. When it rains we can refer to the book and not only say, "Wouldn't it be nice?", but we can say "How can I get these things to come about?".

Another saying is "The best way to get the future you want is to create it".

Well you can create you future.

Henry Ford dreamed of cars for every one. His dreams and his future came true.

Bill Gates dreamed of a computer in every home. He dreamed it and he is getting there.

The Wright brothers dreamed of Flying in a heavier than air machine. Next time you are looking at clouds see the traffic.

They made their dreams come true.

Martin Luther started his greatest speech with the words "I have a dream".

Make sure you have dream.

You can make your dreams into reality.

Something to do now

Create your dream book and record your first dream session.

CHAPTER 16
Reasons

It has been said that if the "Why" is important enough the "How" will find itself.

Now that you have your list of Dreams you need to check them out to see if everything should be on the list.

I encouraged you to dream wildly and here I am asking you to take a second look!!

This is not because I am trying to limit what you can have. The only person who can do that is you. I am simply saying before we expend effort on making your dreams come true find out if you really, and I mean really, want them to.

Many people dream of becoming rich otherwise the lottery wouldn't be so popular. For many it will always be a dream as they do not really want to be rich. It would be nice if it happened but they don't want it sufficiently badly.

I am not saying that wanting a thing really badly makes it happen either but there is a great difference between wanting badly and thinking it would be nice if it happened.

It often happens that when dreams are looked at in this way some of them get dropped from the list as unimportant and others get added.

That is fine, because having a dream list is the first vital stage of gaining the success you want and even defining the success that you want.

Your dreams are your own affair so once you have that list and you have taken ownership of your list you are in a great position to ask yourself how you are going to see them realised.

By asking your self "WHY?" you will uncover many things.

For example you may start of with a vague notion that you would like a sum of money, say £2,000,000. Why?

Perhaps it is because you would like a bigger house and garden and a boat and great holidays. Why?

You want a bigger house. Why? Perhaps because you would like to have many house guests on a regular basis, more than can be accommodated in your present house. Why?

Perhaps because there are some people who you really value and who for many reasons you have not seen for years. They may be old school or services friends. But why?

Maybe you have been working so hard that you have not developed friendships in recent years and you hanker for the old good times with your old friends or family you have not seen for years. Why?

Because we are a social animal and we need that contact with people to gain a reflection of our self worth and maybe you have been wondering where life has been leading recently.

You would like a boat. Why?

To go sailing with the family. Why?

Because you would enjoy being isolated with them and then be able to sail into distant ports with them. Why?

Maybe because you woke in the middle of the night and realised that with all the hours you work you never see your family who are growing up rapidly and you yearn for the chance to have them to yourself without interruption. Why?

Because you feel that although you are providing a living for them you are not giving of yourself directly to them and you know the chance will be lost for ever one day.

People who say they want money often do not. After all what use is money unless you have a need for small scraps of paper.

It is the things that money buys that you want and you have your own reasons for wanting the things you want.

With a strong enough reason why you will generate an incredible faith that what you earnestly desire will come about.

The great inventors, industrialists, military leaders all had a sufficiently strong reasons why to carry them through the hard times. You have very strong reasons why you included the things on your personal list and some will come easier than others. The more difficult ones may take a little time but your reason why will keep you on track and get you there.

When you hit an obstacle you may ask yourself questions such as "Is it worth it?". "Why am I doing this?". When you answer that question you will remind yourself not only of why you started out on the journey but also what the benefits of reaching the destination will be.

It may happen on occasion that when you give your self an answer it suddenly does not seem justifiable that you are putting in the effort.

What has happened here is that your ambitions or your needs have changed and that you need to reassess your dream list to see if it is still representative of your life's ambitions.

And that is something which needs to be done on a regular basis. As you gradually start to see your dreams come true you will add other things to your list and maybe knock a few off which are no longer worthwhile going for.

The way to check them out is to ask that marvellous question WHY?

Something to do now

Look at your dream list and write the reason why you would like that dream to come true. Make sure that you have asked why enough times to get to the real reason. If your reason for wanting the boat stops at, "Because the Smith's have one", you may need to ask why you need to keep up with the Smiths.

Do not skip this valuable exercise and repeat it often to make sure your dreams are in line with your core values.

CHAPTER 17
Specification

So you have a list of dreams. You have some really great reasons to make those dreams come true and maybe you have added a few dreams and perhaps removed a few from your list.

Full of enthusiasm you are ready to start to make them all come true. And that is great.

A question. What is it that you are about to do with such zeal?

As Aristotle would remind us there is no effect without cause and we will want to know what we need to do to cause the effects which we have called our dreams. What exactly are our dreams? What exactly do we want?

The key word is **exactly.**

Imagine your dreams to be white fluffy clouds. We want to capture them and turn them into reality. How do you catch a cloud?

The answer is to make it more solid. Let us define some specifications about each cloud.

Rudyard Kipling told us of his six honest serving men who taught him everything.

Their names were the only six questions which exist. Where? What? When? Why? How? and Who?

The last two chapters should have gone a long way to answering Why and a fair way to defining What.

Do not underestimate the value of spending some time on this exercise. There are immense benefits from setting a tight specification for each dream.

For a start it is just common sense to have a good picture of your destination so that you will know when you get there. A fuzzy picture will not keep you on track and you may finish up at a place which looks like a bit like your picture but isn't.

Another reason is that you may not get your dream realised in one go. You may work towards it in small attempts. With a vivid picture you will realise that you are building towards your dream as you achieve portions of it. A bit like having the picture on the jig saw box and putting a few pieces together to complete a section of the whole.

So how can we use these questions?

Well let us start by putting a date on each of your dreams.

Someone said **A Goal is a Dream with a Deadline**. How true that is. Once you have decided when it is that you wish to start enjoying the fruits of your dreams you have taken a major step. For a start the clock is ticking and you will know that there is a limited amount of time to complete your project.

This puts you into the frame of mind where you ask yourself "What have I got to do?".

We will save that question for the next chapter. Before we can answer it we need to ask "What does my dream look like in detail?"

For example, suppose one of your dreams is to have a brand new Jaguar, BMW or Mercedes car. You have decided you want it by a certain date. Say two years today or a certain birthday.

That is still a bit of a fluffy dream although we have a date.

Which model is it to be? What colour? What about the interior colour? How about any extra equipment? What size engine? How much will it cost insured, taxed and ready to roll?

When you have answered these questions chances are you will have an excellent picture of this dream which has almost become a real specified goal.

You will need to hold this vision in your mind and look at it often. It will help if you can visit a show room and sit in such a car. Involve all your senses. Smell the leather. Listen to the purr of the engine. Feel the support of the luxury seats and take a test drive. Experience the acceleration and remember the admiring looks form pedestrians as you drive out of the show room.

As a reminder of all of these things take a brochure home and keep it handy so you can look at it often. Maybe tear out a picture of "Your Car" and keep it in you wallet so you can see it when ever you want to. Know that it will be yours. Every day when you turn the ignition key of your present car think of your dream.

Do the same thing with holidays you may wish to take or perhaps a property you would like to own one day.

None of these actions will make your dream come true. There are thousands of disappointed people who have collected pictures of things they want, places they want to go, and have not seen them materialise. But— it is a major step in attainment to have this clear picture of what you want. Merely specifying tightly, converting your dreams to goal, will focus any effort that you subsequently put in.

The fact you have recorded what it is that you want will start to concentrate your mind on what you need to do. The fact that you have had some sort of experience of what the realisation of your dream will be like will spur you on to action.

The date you have set will help you create a schedule to work to.

It is important to express your goals in a positive manner rather than negative.

Let us say that one of your dreams is financial. Maybe to be free of debt. You may have a debt of £4000 that has been hanging around for some time and your dream is to be free of it.

Specify in your Goal File what it is you want to see happen and by when. For example, "It is (date) and I have earned an extra £4000 and settled my debt to xxxx. I am now free of debt".

Do you see that you now have a clear target to aim for. It is expressed in positive terms and tells you exactly what it is you wish to achieve and by when.

You could do the same with a dream of losing weight. Get specific.

"It is the 17th of November, my birthday (8 months ahead). I have lost 2 pounds a month and now weigh 16 stone which is my target weight".

Both of these last examples focus on a positive expression of a dream and allow a vision to be created and held. More than that they create a position from which a defined action plan can be developed and embarked upon. Which is what we will look at next.

Something to do now

Create a Goal Book or File by transferring some of your dreams to it in a specified manner.

Give your self a date for each dream.

Ask the six questions about each dream to turn it into a specific goal.

Create a vision for each goal.

Visit your vision regularly to keep it bright in your mind's eye.

Taste the enjoyment of the attainment and remember the taste until you can enjoy it in full.

Specification

You will be amazed at what will start to happen. You will start to realise your goals, in some cases earlier than you had scheduled. You will then add more of your dreams to your Goal Book and see them fall to your efforts. It is a proven fact that people with written goals achieve more than those with out them.

Remember, if you are not working towards your own goals you are working towards someone else.

CHAPTER 18
Planning and People

When you have such people as Sir Winston Churchill and Alexander the Great on your team there is a tendency to curb the urge to rush into new projects with very little planning.

Alexander is very gung ho and full of enthusiasm but he still likes his ducks in a row.

The entire team are all in favour of converting the Dream List to a Goal list by specifying the details.

One major benefit of having a tight specification is that any large or small project can be viewed as a series of small projects.

If, like me, you suffer from terminal procrastination it is a great help to be able to start something, put it down, pick it up several times and finally complete the task. Only by having a schedule or plan is this possible.

At one time the house and garden would be a museum of projects started and long abandoned in their early stages. I am getting so much better at finishing things now that I take a little time to plan what it is that needs to be done.

Take a goal of your own, maybe a small one just to get your hand in, and simply list all the things that you need to do to fulfil it.

Maybe there are a few blanks, a few grey areas.

Well that's fine. Part of planning is to discover those grey areas and to make them clear.

Take a small project such as putting up a shelf.

Your list may include buying the wood, cutting it to size, planing it and maybe painting it. You then need to fix it to the wall.

Questions pop up.

What size wood do you need? Where is your saw and plane. Do you have sandpaper. Do you have the right size drill and screws and wall plugs?

The point is, that that ten minutes spent on a list of this nature with everything put in the right order can save you hours of trudging to your tool shed or the shops. You may even get bored or run out of time half way through and abandon the exercise.

This simple example can be amplified to cover a goal of any size.

The D Day landings in France during World War II were planned to the last detail and hours of planning and rehearsal went into the project before the operation was launched in anger.

As well as standing for Planning P also stands for People.

You multiply your efforts immensely by involving other people. When we discussed the reinvention of you I proposed that there was more to be gained by concentrating on your strengths than spending vast efforts on trying to become something you were not.

As a Rugby forward I quickly learned that there were faster people in the team than me. Some of them were smaller, some taller.

We all learned that we needed each other if we were to meet and beat other teams. If there were 14 other people my size we could be easily be beaten by a balanced team who had people who could out pace us.

If the team was composed of 15 speed merchants it is unlikely they would have the ball with which too run for most of the game. So having others in the team is good planning.

So when creating your detailed planning list of what needs to be done think who will be drafted in to help with things which you either don't want to or can't do.

As part of your plan you will need to check that these people are available, that they know what is required, that they have bought in to your vision and that they are willing to cooperate.

Your associates will need to take ownership of their piece of the task.

It is essential that they know what it is they are supposed to accomplish. I believe it also helps if they are aware of the overall picture. It helps to have a picture of the vision in their mind as well as your own.

They need to know what resources are to be made available or if they are to provide their own. Do they plan as well as you intend to?

What is in it for them? It need not necessarily be a monetary reward. If the task is one dear to their heart then commitment on their part may be much greater than if they are simply employed to fill a role.

Make sure that your people know what the reward for success is and also what failure to succeed will mean to them and every one else.

A cliché I picked up in my early days of life insurance sales was **"No man plans to fail but many fail to plan".**

The truth in that statement is apparent. Would you deliberately sit down and plan how you could build in failure to your goal list? Of course not. But how often do you sit down and plan how to ensure success.

Let me remind you again of the credo of my company.

design4success™..... .....**because it doesn't happen by accident.**

Planning is about designing how to succeed in reaching your dreams and goals. It is working out every last detail of what needs to be done in order to tick items off the list in your goal book.

Something to do now

Take some time out and choose one of your goals.

Make a list of everything which needs to be done. It may help to break the goal down into stages, sub goals, or tasks.

Don't forget to put on your list the names of people who may be involved and what you need to cover with them.

Note any grey areas and plan how you are to clarify them.

These activities will develop into a plan which will effectively give you a simple schedule of tasks which when put in the correct order will enable you to take simple steps to complete the journey to your goal.

Let us say that by this exercise you came up with a list of 1000 tasks to carry out and the pay off would be the completion of a valuable and long cherished dream. All you have to do is knock down these 1000 tasks one at a time and the goal is yours.

Wouldn't it be great to know just what you have to do?

CHAPTER 19
Action

Kriss Akabusi, Olympic athlete, told me "Nothing happens if nothing happens".

Now I love dreaming and converting my dreams into goals.

I get immense satisfaction from planning details, be it a trip abroad or a major project. Sometimes I get so much out of the planning that it seems unnecessary to actually put the project into operation. It is completed in my mind and I have the satisfaction of knowing it will work.

There is only one snag. The pay off is not real. I have never banked one penny from a property development idea I sketched out and planned but did not carry out.

How many times have you had a great idea which you shelved only to find out later that someone else did it? It used to happen quite often once and it happens to me every day now. The good news is that these days it is because I have so many ideas come to me and I am choosy about the ones I put into action.

There is that key word.

ACTION

As we know the benefit of dreaming and converting those dreams to specific goals (having of course decided that we have a good enough reason to get that far) we should have a list drawn up during our planning process of all the things we need to do.

Aristotle will tell me that if I wish to see the effect of my dreams and plans I must cause it to happen.

He is backed up by Churchill who sends out memos with the instruction "Action this day" written on them.

In his seminars Anthony Robbins tells us "Massive Action equals Massive Results".

This is so true and it is also true that little action gets little results and no action gets no results.

This does not mean that little action is not a good thing and that little action is useless.

Take a look at nature. The wonder of a honeycomb or an ants nest. The nest of many birds, the construction of a beaver dam are all examples of large undertakings finalised by the completion of hundreds, maybe thousands of little tasks.

We can learn from this. Some of our major projects for which we have created a plan may require a thousand steps to complete. The task may seem daunting in its entirety but if we break it down into sub stages it becomes a lot easier to handle.

Even tiny projects sometimes are easier if broken down.

Let us return to that shelf. Imagine that you have been promising to put it up for a couple of years. Through your plan of construction you realise that why you have not done it was simply because you never had the wood or a drill the right size for the bracket screws.

Your plan included buying these and probably your first action would be to measure up and then go to the store to buy what was required.

You decide on 'action this day' and you go to the shops. Now the shelf still isn't up but you are a couple of stages nearer. Tomorrow you decide that you are going to cut the wood to size and smooth it. You allow half an hour for this, check that you know where your tools are and relax.

The next day your shelves are ready to put up. You have planned the next stage and so at the weekend you take just an hour to take the shelves, the brackets and screws, your drill and power lead and level from the tool shed into the house (all in one trip) and bingo, an hour later the project which had remained a dream for two years is complete in about three hours total.

What happened?

Having taken the time to think about this and made a plan by creating a list of things to do you simply set about doing them in a structured and efficient way. You took action.

This is how all projects, large or small, get done. It is action and it does not have to be action in one enormous tiring surge.

So how can we help ourselves to take action?

The answer is through scheduling.

When I was playing rugby regularly one thing which never was left undone was my presence on the pitch during the game. Long before I kept a diary, burned into my brain, would be the time and date of the next game. I had scheduled the game and from that came the scheduled time needed to get to the ground and change. From that came the time to eat and leave home.

We will talk about time in a later chapter but the message in this chapter is that to get things done you need to plan when you are going to do them and then do that. DO THEM.

All achievement is about doing something. An achievement is creating a change in a situation. You have already designed what the new situation should look like. You should have had a little taster of what it will mean to you when it arrives through your visualisation but it will only be a taster until it is done, and the only way it will be done is if you do it.

Action

So it all boils down to you taking action. It all revolves around you having a "Things to do list" and having a pen ready to tick off the individual tasks as they fall to your action.

If you have never used a list, apart from the shopping list, you will not have experienced the incredible satisfaction of putting those ticks in. It is infectious too. I know I am not alone in this as many people have told me that they will often start their daily list off with a task they have just completed so that they can reward themselves with a tick. It may be cheating a little but look at it this way.

It may be a form of Pavlovian conditioning. Certainly for me a list with a few ticks on it urges me to get on and action the list some more and collect a few more ticks.

The thing about action is that it takes you nearer to the goal. Just a little action leaves less action to take. No action leaves all the action still to do.

One year when I was doing my New Year resolutions I decided that I wanted to have £1000 saved up by the end of the year. This was a lot of cash to someone fresh out of school.

At that time there were 240 pennies to the pound and 4 farthings to each penny. I calculated that 1,000,000 farthings would be close enough to my target and sat down to think how I could do it. I knew I had some loose change in my bedside locker and found that I had the equivalent of 178 farthings. I put this in a tin and resolved that the only reason it would come out would be to put it in the bank.

Now this still left 999,822 farthings to find but I had a year to do it and somehow 999,822 seemed a lot more manageable than 1,000,000. Boy did getting rid of one comma encourage me.

2739 farthings a day also seemed quite a daunting prospect as well but there ought to be some way to do it.

Well, by the end of the year I hadn't made it. In fact I made just over half way. I did, however, have over £500 saved up which was a load more than I had started out with and was over £500 more than most of my friends had saved. It was a lot of cash in the late 1950s.

How did I do it? I got a job. I played in a little rock and roll band. I didn't buy a motor bike. I didn't smoke or drink loads of beer and I saved regularly. Every Saturday morning I visited the Building Society and put in my weeks savings. I took pleasure in seeing the balance build up and I never withdrew a penny. I discovered compound interest. Did I miss out on some fun? I don't think so and if I did I've made up for it since.

Apart from the satisfaction of the achievement of accumulating the balance I learned a valuable lesson which I must confess I forgot from time to time in the next thirty years.

ACTION GETS RESULTS

Something to do now

> Make sure you have a diary or planner. Put in the deadlines of the goals you listed for completion this year.
>
> Put in the deadlines for the sub goals of your longer term projects you have planned to start this year.
>
> Make a list of the things you intend to have finished this month. From this list, identify what you need to do on a weekly basis.
>
> Make sure that the key details are logged in your diary or planner. Before you go to bed each night write a list of things you must do tomorrow.

DO THEM!

CHAPTER 20
Commitment

One of my trusty tools is my faithful Roget's Thesaurus. Before writing this chapter I thought I would take a look at Commitment. It was with some surprise that I found no such word. The dictionary wasn't much help either, seemingly being concerned with sending people to prison. OK so perhaps I need to update my library.

What was quite interesting however was that in the Roget's there was an entry expanding on Commit (oneself).

Looking this up lead to the word promise. Under this word were several references which I feel nicely summed up the essence of Commitment.

How about 'pledge, undertaking, word of honour, vow, affirmation, guarantee and obligation, for starters'?

These portray to me what is involved in Commitment.

Gandhi's actions and those of his followers in wresting back India from British control whilst refusing to resort to violence demonstrated Commitment.

Churchill's speech about fighting on the beaches and finishing up with "We shall never give in" is another great example.

Roget goes on to mention 'bind, pledge, take upon oneself, bound and honour'.

The general feeling I got from reading these words is that Commitment is an extremely personal thing. The sense of obligation came shining through. Obligation to whom?

Well at first sight a promise may seem to be given to another but on deeper examination if you let someone else down it is you who will suffer the most.

If I say I will be somewhere I like to be there. There was a time when I found it difficult to say NO. I would say OK, I'll try. This meant NO only I wasn't brave enough to say so. Later on when I didn't do whatever it was I said I'd try and do, I then not only had the problem of making up an excuse but I also had to deal with the inner guilt of having let someone down. Soon after came the realisation that I had in effect told a lie in the first place.

I have learned since that it is much better to deal in a completely honest way when it comes to making promises and now my rule is to not make promises I can't keep and to do my utmost to keep to promises I have made.

And that turned out to be the basis of Commitment as far as I was concerned.

When I have identified my goals, worked out the plan and scheduled my action I commit to carrying it out. I make a promise to me that I will see it through.

Take this book for example. Like many people I know who want to write a book I had the concept in my head. It was not a great chore to plan the chapter structure and to set a deadline to have it all written.

In my case I decided that if I wrote a chapter a day on my designated days I would meet my deadline.

There were several days where I did not feel like sitting at the keyboard. There were other days when attractive diversions entered my life. I had made a promise to myself and I was not going to let me down. As I type this sentence it is a lovely sunny day, (about only the third this year) and as I look out of my study window I can see the grass growing by the second. If I am honest with myself I would rather be outside on the mower but that would mean being dishonest to the promise I made myself.

I have made the pledge to finish this chapter by 9.00 am, and I will.

Commitment is also about the intensity of action and the promise to carry out that action.

There are some great phrases in the Roget and in the section open at the minute I see "In for a penny in for a pound".

How many times has a venture failed through a half-hearted attempt at it? The tragedy is that the difference between success and failure is often quite marginal.

Brian Tracy points out that the famous 80/20 rule applies to achievement as in almost everything else. He says that 20% of a project gets completed with the first 80% of effort and the final 80% comes with 20% of effort.

I have seen this rule operating in property renovation. No progress seems to take place at first and suddenly it all comes together at once.

When you are making out your schedule and your plan it is vital that you make true promises to yourself about seeing the project through. Remember it is that vital final stage which will bring the noticeable results.

A great motto that just about every successful person has adopted is

"IF IT IS TO BE, IT IS UP TO ME".

Doesn't this say it all?

In the final analysis who has got more interest in seeing your dreams come to fruition than you?

As we discussed in the last chapter you will have other people involved with your projects and it is a difficult thing to get them to have the same commitment as you. If they have more you should be asking some serious questions of your self.

The way to get a Commitment from other people is to make sure that they not only can see your vision but that they buy into it. They need to feel that their part is just that. They should take ownership of their part and as we said should reap the reward of completing their required tasks.

Peter L. Hirsch in his book Living With Passion asks his readers to pose the question to themselves "Will my children (and if you don't have kids, use your parents or spouse) ever starve to death?

Take the question seriously.

He has never met anyone who said anything other than, "No, not ever, not a chance".

The interesting thing is that no one has any proof when they make the statement. It is made without thinking. It is made without evidence; it is made with the certainty that it will never happen.

How is that possible?

Because it is a statement made with absolute commitment.

This demonstrates to us another characteristic of this thing we call Commitment.

It is nothing to do with HOW whatever we have decided to do will be achieved. It is all about doing it **no matter what.** Remember the penny and the pound?

Does this mean that you have to die in the attempt. Well not all of your projects have your life at stake.

It is all about doing the best that you can do. In Rugby I never minded losing to a better team if our team had played their hearts out and we could have not done better.

To have played eighty minutes of flat out effort may leave one elated if the result is a win but the satisfaction of knowing that win, loose or draw nothing else could have been done is a far more rewarding feeling which lasts for a long time.

To have not fought all the way leaves a nasty taste and I have seen many a match snatched back from apparent defeat by the team who refused to give in.

Another favourite maxim of successful people is

"Quitters never win and winners never quit".

It is obvious that if you aren't in the game you stand no chance of winning.

Something to do now

Re-read your plan and your diary to see the scheduled actions you are to take.

Make a promise to yourself that you *will* carry out all the stages of your plan and that you will do them on time.

Make a further promise that no matter what the discouragement, you will see each goal through to completion. You know that there will be set backs. You know there will be distractions but you will be committed to sail through them.

Kipling in IF urges us to fill each unforgiving minute with sixty seconds worth of distance run. That takes commitment. Be true to the promises you make to yourself, never quit and you will have discovered COMMITMENT.

Chapter 21
Enjoyment

Remember that taste of your goal achievement when you did the visualisation. Indeed you should have had a taste every time you revisited that visualisation.

Well, the planning and all the hard work have paid off.

Now you can enjoy the fruits of your labours.

If it was merely a case of 'that old shelf, then a cup of coffee', the good feeling from the long outstanding job done at last, and the freedom from the frequent reminders from the spouse are good enough.

If it was the long promised and planned for exotic holiday, well now is the time to enjoy it.

Perhaps you have freed yourself from a long-standing and highly expensive debt. Now is the time to enjoy the freedom of this burden in whatever way you have decided. You will probably never have such a debt again because of all the lessons you have learned in meeting your obligations.

I always plan my celebration as part of my goal. There is nothing like delayed gratification for getting the job done.

Even a small task should have its own reward.

Are you a member of the "We'll just have a coffee before we get started" Club?

I was too once.

Now I insist on getting a few jobs done and then relaxing over a coffee while I check out my next job.

Try it. It brings good rewards in terms of getting routine chores out of the way and helps with the dreaded procrastination.

There is a much bigger but hidden reason for celebrating your successes.

When you visualise your reward as you are setting your goal you are imagining the completion of that particular task. This not only gets your subconscious into work mode, and helps identify the details to be activated, but is also a bit like a magnet drawing you to the end result.

All of this makes for good planning and activity.

The hidden benefit of the enjoyment or celebration of success is that the experience of rewarded and celebrated success can easily be replayed in your mind if you burn it in when it happens. This can lead to an increased confidence in future projects and situations. It can lead to an exit from periods of low energy and feeling a bit down.

The key is to be able to replay the reward or celebration at a second's notice.

It has not been regarded as very British to go crazy on winning. Let us remember that Kipling advises us to treat triumph and disaster just the same but having said that, unbridled joy on achieving a pinnacle can be utilised very positively.

We use a technique called anchoring.

Imagine that you are afraid of public speaking for example and you are required to address an audience of 200 people.

Well, there are a whole load of techniques to learn and maybe you have studied them but you still are under confident that you can deliver.

First thing to do in anchoring is to choose some part of your body as the anchor point. I have chosen a knuckle on my index finger which I press with my thumb.

The next thing to do is to replay in your mind, and really picture them, some of the successful and happy times in your life when you felt full of confidence. We all have them stored away.

Now as you revisit and relive these moments associate them with your anchor point. So as I remember some past triumph I press that knuckle with my thumb.

Pretty soon that simple action becomes linked to the feeling of success, confidence and celebration. Just try it and see how it works for you.

It will not be long before you can recall these sensations at will in just a second. The resulting boost will enable you to approach any situation with renewed vigour, energy and confidence.

So here you are full of trepidation at making your first speech. As you walk on stage you activate your anchor point and the confidence you had gained in previous successful situations will come flooding back to you.

Of course, as you achieve future success, and triumph over obstacles you will reinforce this facility by anchoring your new successes to your anchor point.

As you walk off the stage to the applause you lock the moment in by anchoring it. As you receive the congratulations from the people who pat you on the back after your speech you anchor that feeling for replay at a later date.

I have told this secret to hundreds of people and when I see them some time later they nearly always tell me it has made a real and positive difference in their lives.

Top sportsmen use this technique all the time.

If you have ever seen a rugby match where the goal kicker is going through his routine you can see it in action.

He has practised hundreds of times placing the ball on the ground, taking his steps backwards, visualising the ball going over the bar and through the posts. He takes a few deep breaths, steps forward, swings his leg and lets his sub conscious do the rest.

When the ball goes over he will anchor that moment and replay the scenario every time he takes a kick in a match.

Have you seen tennis players punch the air when they win a point? Have you seen them clench their fist and give themselves a good talking to when they miss a point.

Well the punch in the air is a celebration and an anchor point. So is the clenched fist. Rather than replay the bad shot in their mind they replay a past good shot so that they are not feeding a failure command into the sub conscious.

We are creatures of habit and if we constantly dwell on failures we convince ourselves that that is what we are — and how can we then possibly succeed?

If we dwell always on our successes this also becomes a habit and we enjoy more success in the future. There, I said it again. Enjoy your successes and you will enjoy more in the future.

Something to do now

Do not have that coffee yet

Make sure that as part of your goals you have promised yourself a reward for hitting it.

Schedule your rewards.

Always take your rewards.

Choose an anchor point.

Revisit some former successes and anchor them.

Commit to anchoring every future success.

Use your anchors whenever you need a boost.

Commit to enjoying and celebrating your successes.

Do what you enjoy and enjoy what you do.

Now have that coffee.

CHAPTER 22
Pressure and Stress

When I was in charge of a sales team in the mid to late '60s it seemed very important that we all met our sales targets.

The times were expansive and our band of young men had boundless energy to apply to the task of increasing sales.

We were very innocent as to the more sophisticated management and motivational techniques which abound today. Indeed they may not have been available.

In our crude way someone with a target of a £1,000,000 orders would divide it by 52 and then by 7 to arrive at a daily production figure.

There was no real need to have any other form of incentive than the need to be seen performing to the level that the rest of the team were plus the true salesman's desire to be number one in the league table.

We did at that time start to consider the material rewards of hitting the target and several of the team decided they wanted the latest Jaguar, Ford, MG or whatever the particular favourite was. Some even went to the lengths of visiting the showroom to see their chosen model. Early visualisation if you will.

The first thing we discovered was that those who had applied the formula of 52 and 7 would fall behind on their target unless they worked weekends. This was no big problem as a little extra effort on Monday through to Friday put this right. Holidays were a bigger problem, presenting bigger catch up situations, so a few decided to do away with holidays.

It may have been the 'Sixties' or it may have been that the spouses of our sales force got tired of not seeing their men, but we had a lot of broken marriages.

Many of the salesmen complained that their wives did not understand that all these hours were being worked for the sake of the family. Maybe they were. However the wives appeared to regard themselves simply as providers of clean white shirts on a seemingly never ending basis to a lodger who was rarely at home.

Whatever the reasons it was bad to see so many marriages go wrong. Most of the salesmen found new wives as did the wives find new husbands but the question will always remain "Did it have to be that way?".

The answer is most definitely a resounding NO.

If we think of the Mexican fisher man story we can see that maybe it is not necessary to get involved in the rat race at all. Having said that most of us do want to improve our situation and are prepared to work hard to achieve the change.

The question is how to achieve it and keep a sense of proportion. The answer is balance.

Stephen Covey is part of my DR SPACE™ because he wrote the marvellous best selling book "The Seven Habits of Effective People".

Before I read the book I had been searching for years to find a way of getting a balance in my life where earning money was not the be all and end all. Where I could have my family and friends in their rightful position in my life.

I needed to strike a balance between thrift and spending. I wanted to retain my health and fitness yet work as long as was necessary to achieve my goals. I wanted time off to recuperate yet I wanted that time off to be guilt free. I wanted to be serious about my work and yet not lose the enjoyment of life. Spike Milligan just would not approve of a lack of humour.

I read Stephen's book with the intention of getting some management tips on how to run a more efficient business.

What I discovered was a way to run a more efficient me. A more balanced me.

I realised that to have a truly balanced life it was necessary to actively promote every area of my life because if not the imbalance would try and self-correct.

A simple example is that burning the candle at both ends for the sake of business may help the bank balance but not your health, family and social life. Something breaks sooner or later.

With the guidance of Stephen Covey I developed my **Five Pillars** on which to balance my life.

I have a simple concept which says that unless my pillars grow at the same rate then my world will get out of balance.

Each of my pillars demands that I pay attention to its maintenance and growth or my world will not be on the even keel I want.

External demands mean that it is not always possible to attend to each pillar every day or sometimes every week but that is not important. The system has a little slack in it as you will see.

My **Five Pillars**, and we discuss each in subsequent chapters are:

> Family and Friends
>
> Fitness and Health
>
> Fun and Entertainment
>
> Finances and Prosperity
>
> Function and Career

They are not in any particular order as they are all equally important. The main thing is that I have recognised them as being the supporting structures of my world and that I work on them all as required so that in the short, medium and long term they do not get out of balance.

By all means put yourself into my shoes for a moment. Or simply borrow my five pillars for your own. See if they fit. If not define your own.

Simply look at your dream list and see if the achievement of any one of your goals and the way you intend to reach it would damage one or more of the pillars. See also if reaching your goal would enhance the pillars.

From this exercise you may find that in order to maintain a balance you may have to readjust the order in which you go for your goals. You may need to get fit and take some time out with the family before attacking a particularly time demanding project.

You may need to sacrifice a bit of fun and entertainment to concentrate on a short term financial project.

At least if you are aware that you are neglecting some area of your life then you can do something about it.

We will look at the pillars in detail but in the next chapter we will take a quick look at Time.

In essence what we have said in this chapter is that you will get more out of life if you spend your time in the correct proportion and on the correct things.

Only you can decide what those proportions and subjects are. Only you can decide what is the correct balance.

A great place to start is the realisation that life has many facets and you have several roles to play.

Something to do now

Take five pieces of paper and write a pillar at the top of each. If you feel you want to add or subtract a category feel free to do so.

As part of your overall planning make a list of all the roles you play. These may include, Father, Mother, Son, Daughter. Provider, Boss, Employee, Sportsman, Investor, Cinema or Theatre visitor, Skier, Gardener, Charity Worker, Speaker, Teacher, Student.

At any one time you may be in a different role. It is important to be in the roles at the right time and not to ignore any of them.

Put each of your roles under one or more of the pillars. It is sometimes possible to fulfil a role in different situations. For example you may be a teacher both to your children and your employees. Use the pillars as a prompt for your roles and your roles as an example of a role in another pillar.

Add to the list any roles which you feel you would like to have. Imagine which area of your life you would like to perform the relevant role and put it under that pillar.

We will be using this list to help you plan your self development and also to create the balance you must have to ensure that you achieve your goals with out stress and with maximum balance.

CHAPTER 23
Time

In my seminars I often ask who would like more time. Nearly every hand goes up.

Tough! Because all there is is all there is. People may be born in different places with different health and diverse opportunity but the only thing we have in common is 24 hours each and every day.

Then I ask if any one would like to manage time. Again the hands go up.

Tough again! Time steadfastly refuses to be managed. It ticks by at the rate of one second per second, one minute per minute, one hour per hour and one week every seven days.

No matter what we do we can not stop the relentless march of time.

The next question is who would like to manage themselves better so as to make full use of the time available. The hands go up no less enthusiastically and I detect the sense of understanding starting to creep through the group.

Speak to any one over 45 and they will tell you that time seems to pass quicker than it used to. We know of course that this can not be the case. The planet doesn't speed up in rotation as we age. I think this apparent speeding up is something to do with the ratio of time left to time passed.

Young children have a large chunk of their life left compared to what has passed. An Octogenarian may not be counting but knows that the major part of life has gone by.

The pace of modern life has definitely speeded up and there seems to be an ever increasing demand on time.

So what can be done?

If you knew your time was limited to just a few years would you spend it in a different way than you are at present?

Well I have news for you.

Your time *is* limited to just a few years and you do not know for certain how many.

Yet still we procrastinate.

There is some good news though. By using the DR SPACE™ process you should be able to have identified just what it is you wish to accomplish with your time. You should have identified what it is you need to do and you should have got yourself a diary to schedule this activity.

Let us just look at some strange things which happen to us when we start to schedule things.

We start to get deadlines. We get behind. We feel guilty and sometimes stressed. We start to work on non productive tasks and even postpone them for fear of not doing them correctly.

We suddenly realise that a holiday is coming up and so get three weeks' work done in a week, become stressed out and then fly away for two week's escape, only to return to a mass of mail or whatever.

The heads I see from the front of the room always nod at this part of the seminar. Who hasn't been there?

Well, if we can get three weeks' work done in one week before we go on holiday why don't we have more holidays? Seriously. I'm not joking.

Since I started to schedule my time off as the first item in my diary each year I find that my output has gone up during the time I do work. Not only that but I enjoy my time off more as I am better relaxed and I return deeply refreshed.

As I have confessed elsewhere I could procrastinate for England. I could win the Olympic Gold medal only I would put off collecting my medal.

Why do we procrastinate? I believe there is more than one reason. We may not like some of the work we have to do and so it is natural to put it off. We have all been there I bet.

As humans we have choice and that is the secret to this type of procrastination. Why do something you don't like? Well there is only one reason and that is because if you do not do it there would be a penalty to pay which is more uncomfortable than the task you are putting off. I hate routine administration, but I know if I don't tax and insure the car when they become due; if I don't complete my tax return and pay my tax on time, I will suffer big time sometime.

So I **choose** to do those jobs rather than procrastinate and suffer the consequences.

Another type of procrastination stems from being schooled that we should never make mistakes. Not starting for fear of failure is a much bigger mistake than not starting at all. If you plan correctly you will reduce the chances of mistakes and if you do not eliminate them at least you will have learned a lesson.

One of the biggest sources of procrastination comes from the realisation that the particular job is too large to finish in one go. It may be that the end picture has not even been visualised. Well, you now know all about the benefits of visualising the end result so, that shouldn't apply to you. But what about this 'large task syndrome'?

Just get started. It doesn't matter if you put the task to one side as long as you pick it up again. I read somewhere that the definition of a good pilot is one who has the same number of landings as takeoffs. You will have conquered procrastination when you complete the same number of jobs as you start.

You can do this by starting and restarting until you reach the point where the next time you start will be the last time.

I have so many ideas and love starting a new project. This I confess has led me to leave quite a few projects unfinished but I get better and I schedule my revisits to my older projects on a regular basis and now I know that one day they will be complete. Steady progress and effort applied regularly will crack any problem.

The key thing to remember is that it is your time and no one else's. You must decide how you want to spend it and unlike money it can not be saved for use later.

As a generalisation we tend to not regret the things we have done. We did them at the time with the best of intentions and dealt with the result good or bad.

What we do regret are those things we left undone. When the moment passes it seldom returns.

Something to do now

Commit to using your time wisely. Make a few small changes to your schedule and get used to them before making larger ones.

I have a friend who decided to get out of bed fifteen minutes or so earlier than he had been doing.

The extra two hours a week was sufficient to enable him to get a load of niggly little tasks done before breakfast which he claims set him up for the day.

Make a list of abandoned projects that you would still like to see finished and make as many restarts as it takes.

Book all your holidays and time off in your diary and commit to honouring these commitments. Promise yourself that you will work effectively and efficiently in between times so that you can treat your time off as a reward and refreshment time.

Constantly review your diary in retrospect to see where you can improve. A little change every day will add up in time.

And don't forget to take time to write that list of things to do. It is probably the single biggest time tool you can ever employ.

CHAPTER 24
Family and Friends

I said earlier that for a balanced life it was imperative to work on all five of the pillars on a regular basis and that therefore they were equally important.

I hold this to be true as far as the work and effort goes.

If I were told that my last moment was imminent and that balance therefore was no longer important I am fairly certain that I would be promoting Family and Friends as my critical pillar.

You may differ in your views and you will have your own values but if I look at the other four values, with the possible exception of health and fitness, I can always make up for lost ground as far as Fun, Finance and Career are concerned.

There are always opportunities to get richer, to take some relaxation and entertainment time and to become creative as regards employment. Even deteriorating health and fitness can be addressed up to a point.

However the sad fact is that we humans are mortal and our span is limited.

There have been loved ones in my life who have gone. There are old friends I have not seen for too long. There are members of the family I do not see frequently enough. There are friends who are of more recent acquaintance who I would really like to see more of and develop the relationship.

If I do not do some thing about it the opportunity may be gone forever.

Is it the same for you?

Now I am far from being a negative and pessimistic person but facts need to be faced.

Marcus Aurelius, in his kindly way, is always pointing out that we are not everlasting. Spike Milligan despite his fantastic sense of humour has had his moments of depression and takes a wicked delight in reminding me of my mortality from time to time, even if he does make me laugh for a moment at the thought of my own demise.

Which of your family and friends are really the ones who you value the most?

Try this exercise and you may be surprised at the results.

Imagine that as of this very minute you were never to see any of your family nor any of your friends ever again.

How do you feel?

Now a genie appears and grants you a wish. You may choose one person to have back.

Who do you choose?

The genie says he was short changing you and that you may have another wish and you can choose up to twenty of your family to have returned to you.

Who do you add to the list now?

The genie is in benevolent mood and he tells you that under genie union rules he has to give you three wishes anyway so perhaps you would like to extend your list to your closest friends.

Who is going to be on your list?

The purpose of this exercise is to try and help you evaluate the people who are really important to you.

When I constructed my list I realised that there were so many people who I had not seen for ages.

The second realisation was that I was spending time with some people who were not contributing to my life at all.

It became a simple choice. Who would I rather be with?

That answer was easy and I resolved to see more of the people I wanted to see. I also decided to cut a few people out of my life who I didn't want to see. An unexpected benefit came from this.

I found out that some of those last people had been having an incredibly negative effect on me. I found that they had been sapping my energy and almost in some parasitic way had been draining my resources. In fact in a very short time I found that my income doubled and then trebled and then quadrupled as my circle of companions became undiluted with these negative people.

Another thought also occurred.

Why hadn't I seen more of the people I really wanted to see? Here the answer was more complicated. In some cases it was because I hadn't either contacted them or had been unable to meet them at their invitation and in others I had taken no initiative due to other demands on my time deemed more important.

Some of my best and strongest relationships seem to have a common link in that contact is made in an alternate way. One time I will suggest we meet and other times they will issue the invitation. It probably works out 50/50 but sometimes I make the running for a while sometimes the boot is on the other foot.

So that one was easy to remedy. Having constructed my list of people it was a simple matter to schedule in a few contact sessions. In fact I am now at the stage where I am getting ready to revive a few old relationships.

What if the other person doesn't feel the same way?

Well that of course, is their choice.

In some cases I am sure that there will be no problem and when I make some overdue contact the response is more often than not that the other party felt that they had been remiss in not making contact earlier and that as a matter of fact they were on the verge of doing so.

In other cases there may be some emotional reason for holding back. There may be a reason why the other person has not taken the initiative for so long.

Again it was Stephen Covey who introduced the concept of Emotional Bank Accounts to me.

He says that in every relationship there is a kind of bank account on each side and deposits and withdrawals can be made, but that these are not monetary they are emotional.

Imagine you have a disagreement with someone and the situation gets vitriolic. Things may be said that are regretted and the relationship is damaged. In other words large emotional withdrawals have been made.

Let us say that you were in the wrong. Your account would be more withdrawn than that of the other person who perhaps acted as a true friend and may have even tried to accept your anger and perhaps tried to deflate the situation.

Perhaps you are so riled that the next time you met the same thing happened. You have now made a couple of withdrawals. Depending on the strength of the relationship your account may be reaching your overdraft limit.

Unless you make a deposit, perhaps in the form of a sincere apology for your behaviour and maybe a sincere thank you to the other person for being such a tolerant friend the next clash could cause your account to be closed with a hefty debit balance remaining on the records.

If you have borrowed money and not paid it back would you expect a further loan from the same source?

If you have been wronged then your account would be in credit with the other person and his would be debited. He may need to make a deposit before you are willing to resume the relationship.

With deep and true friendships and to a lesser degree in new relationships no actual account exists. Subconsciously everything is being totted up. With a trusted friend no account is kept because you have both demonstrated in the past that accounts are kept in balance.

So if you really want a balanced life and you have, for whatever reason, been making more withdrawals than deposits perhaps it is time to do something about it.

Your Family and Friends are of value to you and you are of value to them. In the final analysis you may find that the very reason you are building your other pillars is for the people in your life. It would be a pity if they got out of your life before you had time to deliver.

Something to do now

Make a list of all the good people in your life.

Make a commitment to contact them and tell them that you value their input to your life.

Make a date to see them or schedule more regular contact, even if it is only a short telephone call on a regular basis.

Make a list of people who are draining you and who contribute absolutely nothing to your life. Make sure this is the case. You may be receiving some kind of benefit not at first apparent.

Commit to take no initiative to contact them and think of a strategy for dealing with them if they invade your life.

Work on valuable relationships to increase their value by being of value to the other person.

Be aware of the emotional bank account but do not be mercenary about it. Make deposits and your sub conscious will let you know if the other person's account is in the red.

CHAPTER 25
Fitness and Health

The hardware which is us is our body. To get the best out of life it needs to be maintained in a fit state and not abused.

Do you have difficulty in achieving this? Do you like the good life too much?

The body, it has been proved, has a vital link to the mind and vice versa. The mind, like the body, is in need of suitable nourishment and exercise. Without these deterioration and lack of growth occur.

There is a third area of fitness and health and that is the spirit.

We can come to some form of agreement as to what constitutes the body and mind and spend many an hour discussing what we mean by the spirit.

The word spirit has many connotations ranging from religious to alcoholic and from courage to ghost.

In the context of this chapter I see spirit as something certainly non material. It is something requiring nutrition and exercise in the same way as the mind and body but these being of a different nature.

The spiritual needs differ from person to person in a way that the body needs do not.

Perhaps if we look at the needs of the Body, the Mind and the Spirit we will see these differences.

The Body

Very few people learn the value of a healthy body until theirs starts to deteriorate.

As youngsters filled with boundless energy and a horizon of time and mortality that is far in the distance we assume that this natural health will continue. The arrogance of youth leads us to believe that we will be invulnerable to the ravages of time and bodily abuse.

We have proof. Late night parties and the like, burning the candle at both ends, is no problem. Recovery is pretty instant and the dose can be repeated.

Later on in life we notice that our performance is not what it used to be. A late night can take some time to recover from and our energy levels and endurance seem to decline. Whereas we could at one time eat whatever we liked and still retain our youthful shape a chocolate bar seems to be applied straight to the waist and hips.

In the worst case the decline is so bad that having expended all available energy in removing the chocolate bar wrapper there is hardly enough energy left to point the remote controller at the television to change the channel!

OK. Hopefully you are nowhere near that state but some of the other words may have seemed familiar.

So what can be done?

How about asking DR SPACE™ and using the system?

What is your dream? If you are in your forties or fifties for example would you like to do all the things you could do in your twenties? I would but I know that that is an impossibility. Forty eight years of rugby have left me with so many damaged joints and bones through injury that I could never emulate those days. However, I can be the best I can be.

What would be my reason for being fitter and healthier?

It is amazing how most people will have their car serviced regularly, make sure that it gets the correct fuel and lubrication, and have any repairs or replacements done as soon as they become required. Yet these same people will feed themselves the wrong fuel and lubricants, not have a regular check up and carry on abusing damaged body parts to the detriment of currently healthy ones.

My reason for taking better care of my body is that when I ceased to play rugby and stopped training my weight increased, my stamina declined, my strength declined and my mind also slowed down.

I wished to arrest this and recover as much of the former physical me as I could.

Specifically I have set weight and performance targets.

The planning was easy. A three part plan consists of dietary vigilance, an exercise programme and the indulgence in healthier practices and the elimination of non healthy ones.

The planning was easy. The practice and action less so.

It takes a lot of discipline to keep to a healthy diet and there are many temptations and pitfalls on the road to healthy eating.

Bren is particular about what she buys in the shops and takes great care to balance our diet. Alas we both are fond of chocolate and biscuits and we succumb more than we should. I have a passion for jelly babies and when I buy petrol I am often tempted by the packets on sale by the till.

Progress is being made however, and we are lucky to have an interest in gardening and supply ourselves and several of our friends with nutritious fresh organic vegetables.

In our western world we have too much of the wrong sort of food available. In a recent program on the television a family were invited to try and live as did the families of the second World War. As they were denied the modern diet they started to eat the food of the early 1940s. At the end of the experiment they declared themselves to feel much healthier than before. They had to plan more carefully what they were to eat as opposed to what they fancied eating.

The second part of the action was to take more structured exercise. We always try and include walking in our holidays and take time out in the lovely Lake District once a year.

Simply parking the car as far from the office door as opposed to right outside it, taking the stairs instead of the escalator and walking instead of using the car for short journeys all add up.

Joining a gymnasium or exercise club will pay dividends. The pool for swimming, the aerobic machines and the attentions of a trainer to construct a specific program will lead to fitness and elasticity. The weights and other machines, again with a structured program, will generate stamina, strength and energy.

It is a simple matter to schedule a three times a week training session and the benefits become so apparent after the first month.

Like the temptations to the diet there can be many distractions to your scheduled visits so Commitment is required as contained in the DR SPACE™ process.

The Enjoyment part is easy. Even during the training process there is a great physical pleasure in feeling the blood flowing through long disused capillaries; while a long forgotten sense of well being comes from that physical action.

And when you are at the peak of fitness and health for a person of your age you will obtain further satisfaction from knowing that you have opportunities for further pleasure denied to your contemporaries who are gaining their pleasures vicariously on the couch in front of the television.

The Mind

As the body tends to seize up through lack of use so does the mind. As the body will die without food so will the mind.

The exercise of the mind is to think. Television gives us entertainment at the touch of a button but I am sure the mind is no longer stimulated in the same way that it is by radio. There is no need to imagine. It is all done for you.

Talking to many people I find that there is a decline in those who read a book on a regular basis. One of my greatest pleasures is cracking a crossword with a friend over a pint (or two) of real ale. The task of filling in the answers involves getting into the mind of the compiler which in itself is an interesting exercise.

The exercise and development of ones mind is of course a matter of choice as in everything but that choice is stagnation and shutdown or growth.

Anything worthwhile takes effort and we know that we are naturally lazy. The pay off in exercising the brain and the mind may come slowly, but remember the baby steps principle.

Take small regular steps and learn to walk then run. When you open your mind, when you feed it new ideas and knowledge you will generate new ideas pertinent to your situation.

The more you learn the more you will realise that there is so much you do not know.

When you make the decision to learn as much as you can and to keep your mind and your brain in a permanent state of readiness, warmed up for instant use you will be in a position to take advantage of what life has to offer and be able to see ways of seizing it that were previously hidden from you.

The Spirit

There are things which move me in a certain way which I think of as spiritual. They may not do the same for you but other things will.

A particularly awesome mountain panorama, the story of someone who has overcome a serious challenge to achieve out of the ordinary results, a moving piece of poetry and the London Marathon are a few examples.

I am not ashamed to admit that on most occasions when I visit the theatre at curtain call my eyes fill with tears. I can not explain this but know that what I am feeling is my version of a spiritual experience.

Sometimes when I sit on one of the several seats in our garden and catch a particular view through the trees we have planted I get that same feeling.

We love Florence in Italy and some of the sculptures there such as David invoke this feeling again and again.

The Canyons in America have an epic beauty which brings on a feeling which is also experienced by entry into some of the Great Cathedrals of the world.

You may think that this Spiritual feeling is some what passively experienced but I have discovered that it can also be stimulated by helping out others in some way. When we give to Charity it sometimes happens but not always and that I have no answer for at the moment.

Never the less giving to others is something which works and I am not alone in this. We are fortunate enough to have some great friends who support us on occasions when we run functions to raise funds for some deserving cause and they do so not for us, not just for the cause whatever it may be, but because they also have a similar experience gained through giving.

How do I know? Because they have told me so.

So this Spiritual thing can involve actively doing something or passively receiving something.

I have made a decision to actively give and receive.

You will read later of our Charity and what we are doing. This is action.

Sitting and looking at the view is proactive. I decide when I am going to do it and schedule it.

As my father was often heard to quote, "What is this world if full of care we have no time to stand and stare?".

Something to do now

Body

Stop buying junk food. Shop only for healthy food.

Walk more, ride less.

Schedule some exercise and take it.

Join a health club.

Mind

Watch stimulating TV. Read good books.

Challenge your thinking process. Start to think again if you have stopped doing so.

Seek out new ideas. Consider new challenges and think them through.

Talk with your friends about new issues.

Spirit

Take some time out for introspection.

Find things which move you in a way that makes you feel genuinely good. Revisit them.

Read some poetry and find a few favourites. Cry over them if you feel like it.

Be moved by the beauty of Nature. Visit places which move you.

Give to some body else whose needs are greater than yours.

Count your blessings.

CHAPTER 26
Fun and Entertainment

Who needs to make this a Pillar? I do for one.

In an ideal world, according to many people, life would be 100% fun. I am not sure I disagree although I have yet to see the ideal world.

It would be pretty close to this if work was fun and if every contact with another human being was fun and if there were no tragedies in life. Imagine life with no financial problems.

A life with nothing but fun seems great but it may get so hedonistic that in the long term it may become self damaging.

Remember this section of the book is all about achieving balance and so we need to examine what we need in the way of fun and entertainment and how they can be used to assist us in maintaining our balanced life.

At one end of the scale is a life of complete self-indulgent pleasure and at the other a life of total denial. Where do we place ourselves?

As a concept I subscribe to the idea of trying to make every thing I do have an element of fun in it. This is why I have Spike Milligan on the team. Maintaining a sense of humour in adversity helps get through those difficult times.

Obviously if there are disposable unpleasant situations which are not essential to your life then why not ditch them? Even activities which were once fun and entertaining may have ceased to be.

For example I know several people who I have invited to a meeting or function who reply "Sorry I can't come to that. I have such and such a class on that evening".

As we talk further it becomes plain they would rather come to my function because it sounds more interesting than what they have planned.

When I ask them why they don't simply come to mine instead they reply "Well I have paid my subscription and although I don't really enjoy it any more it will be a waste if I don't go".

Now is it a waste? The answer is Yes, but of what?

They have already paid the money and in retrospect that may have been a mistake but why continue to waste the Wednesday evening instead of changing activity and doing something worthwhile?

The whole point of fun and entertainment is that we need it to refresh ourselves for the future stresses we may encounter in the other areas of our life.

There is also another and very important reason to indulge in relaxation and pleasure.

Quite simply **IT IS THE PAY OFF**.

Just take a quick look at your dream list. How many of your dreams (now converted to specific goals) are designed to give you some form of pleasurable reward?

Even if some of your dreams are framed so that they really mean the avoidance and absence of pain of some sort they are actually aiming at a substitute in the form of fun. If any of your planning includes activities which can not be categorised as fun then it is important to have a reward which is pleasurable and which can be enjoyed on completion of the task.

So if Fun and Entertainment are to be a Pillar then they should be given regular and scheduled attention otherwise the old imbalance will occur.

I have a client company whose sales force includes some excellent and hard working young men. They are highly committed to hitting their sales targets and they have good reasons for so doing. The reasons are mainly monetary as they are building homes and families and every pound is of great use to them.

During one of my sessions it became apparent that there was a little stress developing on the domestic front in some cases.

With the salesmen giving all their time to sales not only were the salesmen becoming more exhausted but rare time off was guilt ridden and wives were not getting the opportunity to see their husbands as often as they would like and in a relaxed state.

This was a clear case of One Pillar overload.

I explained the Five Pillar concept and got the agreement of the salesmen that they would take the following course of action.

1) Book a theatre visit and romantic dinner for two.

2) Explain to their wives that a short period of hard work was coming up but at the end of it, having achieved a certain target which would benefit them both and the family, a celebration would occur – just for the two of them.

3) Make an apology that for this brief period the long hours of selling would have to continue but no longer than absolutely was necessary.

The result was that a greater understanding occurred between the salesmen and their wives.

The wives took a greater interest in the achievement of the targets and in some cases even suggested a few leads to their husbands.

The salesmen found that because they were working under less pressure to rush the sale and get home they actually were able to do a better job and closed more sales for higher figures.

When it came time for the reward in the form of the theatre and meal it was greatly enjoyed without the thought that this was time away from the sales arena.

By this time the wives were already asking what the next target was and were busy leafing through the Forthcoming Attractions in the theatre program.

This simple story serves to illustrate the benefits of planning fun and entertainment as part of scheduling your activities.

It is without doubt important to relax to recharge batteries. It is important to take a break from the work place, no matter how much your job is enjoyable, and to stand back to take a view of the rest of the world.

To schedule a reward for completion of an onerous or unpleasant task makes it easier to take the necessary action.

If you make a habit of rewarding yourself for the completion of a goal you may just become a reward junkie. To feed your habit you will need to create success as you only reap the rewards on the back of your successes.

Success does not happen by accident. Why should your fun happen by accident?

Get your fun guilt free as a reward for a job well done. Guilt free?

Fun — isn't that what we are here for anyway?

Something to do now

Choose a task or project you have been delaying getting started on. Choose a reward which you will enjoy when you have completed this task.

Schedule this reward and visualise it. If it involves booking get it booked.

Make sure that your planning and action lists for every one of your dreams contains a reward.

Take some large project and examine it for any sub goals you have created as part of the planning process. Make sure that you have scheduled some appropriate reward for reaching the sub goal.

Remember, success is there to be enjoyed.

Enjoy it!

CHAPTER 27
Finance and Prosperity

Earlier in the book we examined what deeply seated ideas and paradigms were holding us back. Self sabotage is something that can lurk deep within and this applies to prosperity and wealth as much as anything else.

From an early age the majority of us are fed the idea that it is noble to be poor and that money is evil. Many concepts are implanted to reinforce this such as "poor as a church mouse".

In the past it was in the interest of the ruling classes to keep the working classes poor. Indeed the rich got rich and the poor got poorer.

Things started to get better with the industrial revolution, post World War I and even more after World War II. Now in the Information Age it is possible for anyone to become wealthy in a short time.

The old order can be turned on it's head overnight.

Henry Ford, Bill Gates and Richard Branson are just three examples of people who dropped out and who did not complete a full education programme yet became very wealthy.

The first stage in becoming wealthy is to clear out the clutter of those damaging beliefs which stop you becoming wealthy. Money is no more evil than a gun or a knife. A knife in the hands of a murderer is bad but not in the hands of a surgeon.

The fact is that if you have money you can do more things than if you have none. You can have more fun, more security, better food, improved medical facilities, nicer holidays and you can be of more assistance to the rest of the world.

Getting the correct mind set is most important. Some people believe that there is only a fixed amount of wealth in the world and that it should be spread evenly. Well you can not make the poor rich by making the rich poor.

I came across a tiny book some years ago called The Science of Getting Rich by Wallace Wattles. In it he tells us that if we do not have a competitive mind set but a creative one we will prosper and have anything we desire. He goes on to say that it is not necessary to take anything from any one else and that if you have your financial goals firmly envisioned you will steadily work towards them. You will provide services which will benefit others so that what you have created for others will be transformed into the desires of your own mind.

In simple terms it is a win/win mindset and any other option is not a good situation to be in.

So if we want financial stability, prosperity and wealth we can use the DR SPACE™ Process to get them.

We can start by dreaming of the wealth we would like.

We can ask ourselves if we really do want our dreams to come to fruition or are they always to remain dreams. What would we use our prosperity for?

We can be specific by making lists of all the things we wish to have and do including the cost, the income we would need to support our chosen life style, and of course we would not forget to put some dates on these.

We can plan our activities to realise these goals. This may include gaining further qualifications or skills, or actively developing new contacts. It may mean changing a work pattern, perhaps moving from an employed status to self employed. It may mean buying or starting a business.

It doesn't matter what your own solution will be as the answer will come once you have posed the question by being specific with your dreams.

You will take baby steps to accomplish the journey.

If you are in debt as I was when I decided to commit to an action plan this needs to be dealt with. My debts were business debts incurred by my own stupid fault of letting my colleagues commit to financial burdens which became too heavy for me to service when the 'colleagues' decided to part company with me.

Those giving financial advice often advise cancelling debt as a priority above all other financial goals.

I ask two questions. One, can a higher rate of interest be gained than is being paid on any funds which may otherwise be allocated to debt erosion and two, what about living a life?

I have seen many people in debt strive to get out of debt and in the process put themselves in a position where they are missing out on life and the boundless opportunities which are ever present.

My own plan was to first make a list of my debts and I then contacted every one and told them I was on the case. I made promises that I knew I could keep and I kept them.

Second, I made my promises on the basis that I would live on 70% of my post tax income, use 20% to erode the debts and keep to my schedule. Then against conventional advice I saved 10%.

With time three things happened.

The debts were gradually eroded. My income rose with an ever improving life style funded by an increasing 70% of income.

My available cash grew enabling me to take advantage of opportunities otherwise denied for lack of funds. Paying cash for items means paying no interest and saving on the price.

Any one can work a plan like this but of course it takes the next stage of The DR SPACE™ process, Commitment, to see it through.

When you have seen it through the final stage, Enjoyment, is guaranteed because you have no debts, you have a better life style because you can now live on 80% of income and even more opportunities can be taken up due to savings being 20%.

The ultimate goal is to ensure that the savings become investments which can then create a passive income which does not need to be worked for.

The creation of this situation gives total freedom and choice which must surely be the prime dream of everyone.

Something to do now

Make a list of all your assets.

Make a list of all your liabilities.

See if you can improve the return on your assets.

See if you can settle any of your debts which are penal in interest.

Take a look at your income and if you have debts consider the 70/ 20/10 method.

If you have no debts consider the 80/20 method.

Believe that all the money and wealth you could ever wish for exists and that you will discover a way to earn it.

Take independent financial advice.

CHAPTER 28
Function and Career

"Why have I left Function and Career as the last of the Five Pillars?" is a question I am often asked.

The point is that if we are after balance it really doesn't matter which is last or first.

I appreciate the reason most people ask the question though as in modern life the other Pillars are often given a subservient position to earning a living.

As we know, this attitude will only lead to broken relationships, no fun, stress and poor health if taken to extremes.

I have done my share of candle burning at both ends in the name of business and it can only go on for so long.

However, unless we are fortunate to have an inherited fortune, chances are we will need to work for a living.

Sadly so many children never get to become what they once dreamed of being and finish their working life with a feeling of non accomplishment.

I once came across the following little ditty.

> If you keep your nose to the grindstone
> And you keep it there long enough
> In time you'll discover there's no such thing
> As brooks that babble and birds that sing
> These three will all your world compose
> **You, the stone and your poor old nose**

So, the question is how do we get the balance right in terms of having a satisfactory working life and earning enough to do the things we want to do while having enough money to pay for it?

The answer to this is to differentiate between what you are and what you do.

You may have skills, qualifications and knowledge which may be particular to a given profession.

You may have been channelled into that profession or occupation. You may be brilliant at what you do and yet...

You may not be happy. You may not feel that you are fulfilling yourself.

You may be bringing home the bacon but have no time to make a sandwich.

The cost of your high earnings (or low for that matter) may be stress and dissatisfaction with your career prospects.

I believe every job should have a little pressure even if it is only the pressure of maintaining chosen standards and values

A definition of stress I like is –

When the perceived demands exceed the perceived resources.

To avoid the stress, to feel that what you are doing is worthwhile and not just a way of paying the bills you need to be doing what you want to do and to be doing it for a very good reason.

This way you will get enjoyment, a sense of worth, internal recognition and the knowledge that you are working on your own version of success.

You need to assess what you are doing and see how you can make the necessary changes to do what you really want to.

I was an independent financial adviser for thirty years and I took a great deal of satisfaction from helping people buy houses, protect their families against early death and illness, save for early retirement and old age. I was a salesman of course and I earned good money.

The truth is that during those years I got more pleasure from recruiting and training my sales force than selling the policies.

My real satisfaction came from training and coaching people who thought they were stuck in some mundane and boring job and changing them into financial advisers who, through the ethical application of the skills and knowledge they were given by my training, could become wealthy and be providers for their own families in a job they enjoyed.

You may have medical skills for example and be trapped in a pressure job. Could you change what you do and who you do it for? Could you find a different way of applying your skills in a way that realistically helps people in a better way, maybe in different place. How could you do what you do but enjoy it more and with less pressure?

Perhaps you earn enough money but the pressure is so high that it is spoiling the job. Could you work less hours, still have enough money and maybe use your skills on a voluntary basis to help needy people. You will gain so much satisfaction and meet new people. Perhaps this may lead to you being headhunted by an organisation which would pay you even more with increased responsibility, but with a team under you to take away all the pressures. Who knows?

It is vital that you know what you want. Use the DR SPACE™ process to make sure you know what you want in this respect.

Make sure, as always, that your dreams and goals are always integrated and on closer examination you may reach a surprising discovery as I did.

I realised that I was a trainer not a financial adviser. Financial advice was my business. What I did and enjoyed most was the training.

You may be a draughtsman by profession but you may want to use your skills as a creative designer.

You may have nursing skills but you may have a desire to run your own business. Could you use your knowledge to run a nursing agency?

Another of my goals was to be a property owner. This involved owning more than just my house. Financial advice was my business but it paid for my property through the rents the business paid.

Nowadays many of the large brewery companies are in fact property companies with tenants who happen to sell their beer. I have heard it said that McDonalds is in fact the largest property company in the world by the same token but every one thinks they are in the fast food business.

Take some time out and re examine your career. What is your function? You may be a graphic designer. You may want to be an artist. You may want to entertain children. What stops you becoming an animator and creating a famous cartoon character beloved by children world wide? What stops you?

You may be a truck driver delivering meat from an abattoir to the same supermarket every day. You may have a hankering to be a travel writer. Could you get a job driving a truck for a Formula One racing team or a touring rock band? Could you at least get a long distance lorry driver's job with deliveries to different destinations every day so that you would experience different places and so be able to write up your experiences?

No matter where you are right now it is the starting place for where you will finish up. You are the sum of your experiences and decisions to date.

You can not change the past and you can not live in the future.

What you can do is decide where you want to go, what you want to do and how you want to do it.

Whatever position you are in now you must fill it to the best of your ability and when the right opportunity arises you will be able to take it with the blessings of those you have worked with and for.

We are in a constantly changing world and you need to change. It may be a change of occupation on the surface with you still being you underneath.

Brian Tracy likes to tell people he has just met that he knows what they do for a living.

When they challenge him he simply replies that they solve problems.

That is what all of us do in our jobs and businesses. If there were no problems to solve there would be no job. That is why redundancies take place. Because problems which were being solved by people either no longer exist or can be solved by some alternative and cheaper method.

Think what problems you solve. Ask if you could solve them in a different way, for different people or maybe different problems? Could you solve more problems for people?

Be inventive. Ask yourself uncomfortable questions. Scan the papers for stories of people with problems you could solve.

Make a goal of doing what you enjoy and enjoying what you do.

Look into the distance, you have retired. Imagine that you have just met a new friend. He asks what you used to do.

You don't tell him what you did. You tell him what you achieved.

I won't say "I was a Financial Adviser". I won't say "I was a trainer and coach". I will say "I helped hundreds and maybe thousands of people to get what they wanted out of life".

The lorry driver may not say "I was a delivery man". He may say "I helped people experience places they had never been to".

There is a story of someone on a building site who saw three bricklayers.

He asked each of them in turn "What are you doing?"

The first said "I'm laying bricks".

The second said I am building a wall of a house".

The third, with light in his eyes and a smile on his face said "I am building a home for someone".

What are you building? What do you want to build?

Something to do now

Define your profession.

Define what you do.

Ask yourself if what you do is what you want to do.

Ask yourself what problems you solve for people.

Find other problems you could solve for people.

What would be your ideal way of earning a living? Ask yourself, "Why not?".

Chapter 29
Principles and Guidance

So, I had my mentor in the shape of the multifaceted DR SPACE™. I had my 5 pillars for balance.

I had my DR SPACE™ process which I had learned from experience and the test runs on several projects guaranteed success. I could design4success™ and eliminate accidents and cause the end result.

I hope that you have also.

I needed just one more thing and so perhaps do you.

The problem with 10 strong characters such as the mentoring team I had assembled was that there was still the potential for conflicting ideas. As the team was drawn from a time span of nearly two and a half thousand years some of the concepts proposed for instance by Churchill would require explanation before the Ancient Greeks could fully contribute to the discussion.

A possible solution would be for me to act as Chairman and hope that I could simply extract what I needed at any time from the team.

I was uncomfortable with this idea because I would possibly weight advice given to conform with my weaknesses and I would be back where I had started.

It would be a shame not to get the best out of DR SPACE™ having taken such trouble to construct him.

How would a board of directors or a club or any other body deal with it?

Why not have a set of rules, principles or guidelines to act as a kind of funnel for the talents of the DR SPACE™ team.

I set DR SPACE™ the task of selecting as many of these they felt necessary.

The strange thing is that when the list was complete I found that this was not a list to control and guide DR SPACE™ but a code which seemed to cover just about any event which would occur in my life.

By the time I had read it for the twentieth time so many instances from my past had sprung to mind where, if I had such a list earlier in my life, I would have acted differently with great benefits to myself and all concerned.

I decided to adopt the list for the guidance of my life henceforth.

Since then if I feel uncertain about a course of action I refer to my list and I am always pointed in the right direction.

Nothing conflicts and it enables me to manage integrity in everything.

THE LIST

1) Be driven by written, specific, Long, Medium and Short term goals.

2) Integrate all goals with my 5 Pillars for balance.

3) Always be positive and optimistic.

4) Deal with others on a win/win basis.

5) Always respect the dignity of others.

6) Seek to understand before seeking to be understood.

7) Identify and develop projects to link goals and pillars.

8) Plan and schedule all activities including relaxation.

9) Be principle driven in time of stress and conflict.

10) Be truthful and honest with self and others.

11) Say nothing about people behind their backs if not prepared to say it to their face.

12) Under promise – over deliver.

13) Be proactive rather than reactive.

14) Constantly strive to improve mentally, physically and spiritually.

15) Constantly clear clutter mentally, physically and spiritually.

16) Have no debt except for leverage purposes.

17) Break projects down to 20 day sub projects.

18) Action by weekly planning.

19) List activities daily.

20) Compete against self, not others for improved self performance.

21) I will do today what others won't so that I can do tomorrow what others can't.

22) Recognise my goals are not necessarily the goals of others.

23) Always prepare in advance as far as possible.

24) Review goals daily.

25) Be interdependent (via dependence and independence).

26) Delegate properly where delegation is required or beneficial.

27) Start projects, do not postpone and restart many times until complete.

28) Believe in the Law of Abundance.

29) Believe in the Law of Serendipity.

30) Always desire the Best. Always expect the Best.

CHAPTER 30
The Best Self Development Plan
in The World

It is strange how sometimes things are not what they appear. It is also amazing that so many things contain hidden benefits.

For thirty years as a financial adviser I had many business propositions placed in front of me.

Some fell into the category of "pyramid schemes". It was obvious that many would not work and even more obvious that some were illegal. Several were reasonable in concept providing the Company behind the scheme stayed in business.

A few were interesting because of the high potential income although a large majority were structured so that only the top people or early participants would be capable of earning the offered financial freedom.

On deeper examination the dream of residual income based on an entire team working below you so that you needed to do nothing at all suffered from a flaw in that there was always a need to buy a minimum of the product range every single month.

Experience has shown that where this was the case thousands of participants, in an endeavour to keep up their quotas, finished up with cupboards full of unused product purchased only to maintain a position in the plan.

It must be said that many of these older style companies with their motivational techniques opened the eyes and minds of a lot of people whose horizons were limited before their involvement with MLM, Networking, Pyramid Sales or whatever title this business was known as.

Things have moved on and now, as with franchising which once had it's own teething problems, the networking industry has truly come of age.

In my opinion Network Marketing has 'arrived' along with the 21st Century and is a credible and legitimate business which is providing thousands, if not millions, of people with the opportunity to create international businesses from home with a minimal investment and no specialist knowledge.

People, who after a few short years of work alongside their regular employment can enjoy a high residual income, enabling them to enjoy a lifestyle while they are still young enough to enjoy it.

Many become millionaires and thousands more earn that extra income which allows them to transform their lives by settling their mortgages early or cancelling out long term debts.

However, these tangible and material rewards are not the only benefit of being involved in the Networking world.

The association with positive people who know no bounds to their ambitions can lead to personality changes where pessimists become optimists. Eyes long shut to the possibilities which abound are opened for ever. Minds closed by years of negative conditioning are stretched by the realisation that there is a chance at whatever age, whatever education, whatever background to realise long forgotten and deeply buried dreams.

With rising levels of stress doctors, lawyers, accountants, managing directors, pilots are joining the housewives and shop floor workers who are all seeking time and financial freedom.

At last the penny is beginning to drop that we now have a legitimate and regulated type of marketing which is being embraced by more and more companies to distribute their products and services.

It is becoming regarded as a professional business with, in the USA, courses at colleges and universities. Having said that there is no need to have a lengthy learning curve with absolutely no earnings.

With Networking the "apprenticeship" stage can be as little as three months while the earnings of a top surgeon can come within three to five years.

This and the stress factor is why more professionals are joining the industry.

This is good for the industry. Training, marketing, personal development, technical and financial skills together with know-how, are turning this industry into one which any can join and be proud to be part of.

With the new technology available it is possible to build an international business without leaving the home country. Many people however, join for the reason that it gives them an excuse for foreign travel to visit their ever expanding global enterprise.

So, the hidden benefit is the opportunity for personal development, earning while learning.

It is a business which every one should examine and which the majority of people should seriously consider joining.

Whether a fortune is made or not, all those exposed to the business will learn people skills, make friends, make money commensurate with the effort applied and have a new and perhaps broadened outlook

In my own case I realised that the industry has at last come of age and I devote some of my time each week to researching it, enrolling, training and coaching people.

My knowledge of this "Relationship Marketing" industry is growing on a daily basis. My income from this source of activity is commensurate with the results I have achieved and reflects the efforts I have put in to date. As I learn more, as in any new field of endeavour, I hope to get better and increase my earnings.

What I like about the industry is that although I have a support team they are all anxious to see me do better unlike many businesses where superiors are jealous of the growth of subordinates.

I, in my turn, am pleased if the people I have enrolled do better than me.

Why? Because we all have the same opportunity and the nature of the business is that it rewards justly and I ask no more than that.

CHAPTER 31
Give A Man A Net

The whole of this book has been given over to providing you with the knowledge, the skills and the methods to carve yourself a slice of success, whatever that means to you.

I love the definition of success provided by Emerson.

Success

> *To laugh often and much: to win the respect of intelligent people and the affection of children; to earn the appreciation of honest critics and endure the betrayal of false friends; to appreciate beauty, to find the best in others; to leave the world a bit better, whether by a healthy child, a garden patch or a redeemed social condition; to know even one life has breathed easier because you have lived. This is to have succeeded.*
>
> *Ralph Waldo Emerson*

If I had not put such thought into what I wanted to do and achieve and how to get it and if at the end of my life I could say that I had gone even half way to what Emerson says is success, I would still be happy.

Of all the aspects of Emerson's success *to know even one life has breathed easier because you have lived* is the most poignant for me.

It is sad if you have not laughed a lot. Winning the love and respect of others can be hard work and no one can enjoy those petty people who undermine us, often under the guise of friendship.

But is it too difficult to help another soul breathe easier and know in your heart of hearts that if you had not taken that action, then no one else would have?

As I have said elsewhere in this book I am not particularly religious. I do believe in the Golden Rule and I do believe that what goes round comes round.

I also know that true prosperity comes not from hoarding but from giving. I have lost count of the times I have given some small amount for some cause and within hours I have been placed in a position to receive a larger sum back.

Now I do not give simply in order to receive but there is no denying it is satisfying to feel good about helping the less fortunate and having the double hit of getting more back than you gave so that your situation is restored and you are in a position to assist some more.

Truly this has strengthened my belief in the Law of Abundance.

There is an inequality on this planet and all men are not born equal. Many people are the victims of misfortune not of their own making and it is possible, with little effort, to provide a much needed boost in that particular hour of need.

Sadly, much charitable work does not manifest itself in the proffered aid reaching the intended destination. We have all heard of the corruption in some countries which diverts the aid for the needy into the coffers of the evil and greedy. This is a tragedy not only for those helpless people but also for the valiant fund raisers whose efforts may have even worsened the situation.

So my question is "How do we help others needful of assistance and ensure that the aid hits home directly?".

I read somewhere, the bible I think, that if you **give** a man a fish you feed him for a day but if you **teach** him to fish you feed him for life and I thought that this concept was something to work on.

Together with my wife Brenda we formed **GAMAN, Give A Man A Net.**

We raise funds to help people who just need some small assistance to change their lives in a big way. Particularly if they can then help others.

In our buoyant Western economy we little realise how a relatively small sum of money can transform the life of someone on the other side of the world.

For example I was amazed to find that it only takes just £21 to cure a person of leprosy.

Without treatment leprosy can lead to permanent disability and blindness, as well as social rejection and the pain of isolation. I was moved and inspired by the story of Prem a young boy with advanced leprosy. He did not feel the pain of carrying boiling pans and dishes because of his damaged hands.

Prem was cured and his hands were treated but they will never fully recover. He wanted to work and was trained on bicycle maintenance and now is married and can support a family. He was given a net.

Another story tells of a cured sufferer who became a cobbler making special boots and shoes for the damaged feet of his fellow sufferers. One man's net leading to many more nets.

Providing the inhabitants of an entire African village with water will give them the opportunity to improve their lives, even though the cost is less than we pay for water in just one of our homes.

And nearer to home we see guide dogs making it possible for blind people to lead a more full life than otherwise, sometimes taking on employment in some capacity and becoming self sufficient. Yet another net.

These and many other examples of the low cost provision of a net to enable the recipient to fish inspired us to raise and collect funds which could be directed to those in need of assistance, to enable them to assist themselves and others.

We decided that 100% of any money we raised would go directly to either the recipient or to any specialist registered charity which was geared up to deliver the net in an efficient manner.

Any associated costs would either be borne by our company or by one of our associated corporate sponsors.

We are always pleased to receive funds and even more pleased to hear from people who would like to be involved and help us raise funds in some way.

Helping to make even just one life breathe easier is, in my view, success.

CHAPTER 32
Final Words (Almost)

This may be near the end of the book but it is perhaps the beginning of a whole new way of life for you.

I say perhaps because it truly is your choice. I suggest you revisit the book several times now that you are familiar with the structure.

Recruit your own DR SPACE™ from your own heroes.

Use the Five Pillars to get the balance you require.

Use the DR SPACE™ Process to create and finish any project of any size.

Personal Development is a continuous process and it needs conscious effort and the allocation of time. It has been said many times that success is a journey not a destination and success in achieving all you want out of life should be an exciting and stimulating journey.

Of course there are frustrations and obstructions particularly when breaking new ground. You will learn to deal with these and treat them as mere stepping stones. You may even come to the stage where you actually welcome them as sign posts that you are on the right track.

I advise people to give up smoking and they will feel better. I don't just mean giving up tobacco. You will know that you have achieved tremendous progress when you have had your last FAG.

FAG stands for Fear, Anger and Greed.

When you can conquer these three you will have opened up a world of unlimited potential.

Fear is crippling. Learn how to deal with it. Make a list of all your fears and attack them one by one. Start with the smallest by all means and work up to the biggies. You will wonder what you were afraid of once they have been banished. Find a mentor who has no fear of what scares you. Model him or her and use the DR SPACE™ process to eliminate the fear as a project.

Like Fear, **Anger** is an emotion. You will be subject to many circumstances which make you feel Anger but you can learn to do two things.

The first is to examine why a situation makes you angry. Perhaps it is your views conflicting with those of another person's views. Remember that every one is entitled to their view and if you put yourself in their shoes you may gain an understanding. You may realise that the actions of a person which make you angry were in fact well meant. Develop patience as an antidote to anger and remember the old proverb "Act in haste- repent at leisure".

The second is learn to recognise potential situations which make you angry and learn not to act while you are gripped by anger. You are likely to make an inappropriate response whereas a considered reaction is more likely to be effective and less likely to create a worse situation.

Greed is bad and absolutely unnecessary.

Let us get one thing straight to be selfish is human. We all have self interest. As humans we are interested in maintaining our integrity in a mental and physical sense. We act in our perceived self interest although we may not always get it right.

When self interest is applied without consideration for others it becomes counterproductive as alienation of others leads to isolation and the withdrawal of vital support.

Any one who appreciates The Law of Abundance will not suffer from Greed.

There is more than enough air for us to breathe. There is more than enough water for us to drink even if some of it is in the wrong place, or is it the people who are in the wrong place?

There are plenty of resources on our planet to ensure every one lives in comfort or even luxury.

I am not suggesting that all the wealth and resources should be shared out equally. I am not saying that wealth is evil. On the contrary I believe that wealth is good. However, you can not make poor people rich by making rich people poor.

What I am saying is that there is enough to go around and that people who get a chunk of it as a reward for their efforts are surely entitled to keep it but don't take more than you are due and certainly don't take what rightly belongs to another.

It is natural to want to hoard although it is a throw back to a more primitive age. It is prudent to plan for the future. Eliminate greed and you will strike the right balance.

Alongside The Law of Abundance is The Law of Reciprocation and without doubt, the more you give the more you get back.

So plan for the day you have your last FAG.

Final Words (Almost)

I came across a quotation from an anonymous author which expresses and encapsulates DR SPACE™ in my view.

> *"The most basic choice we have in life is whether to bring our creative and expressive energies out into the world in positive or negative ways.*
>
> *No matter what our circumstances, we have the power to choose our directions.*
>
> *In each of us are heroes,*
>
> *Speak to them and they will come forth.*
>
> *We have to live and we have to die; the rest we make up."*

So it is your choice. Positive or negative. You can not fully control the hand you are dealt but you can control how you play it.

Speak to your heroes, listen to them, emulate them.

May your own DR SPACE™ be as good to and for you as has been mine.

Be positive, be generous. Live the life you want and deserve and live it right now.

All the Very Best.

Clive Hall

CHAPTER 33
Designing Your Success

Well, there really are only a few more pages left but it is not the end of the book.

I hope that you have enjoyed reading it and that you were able to relate to my experiences and the solutions I have found.

If this is the case then use the book as a manual and refer to it often as you design your success.

By following the suggestions for **what to do now** at the end of most chapters you will certainly be making progress as far as identifying what you want out of life.

More than that you will have given yourself some good reasons to go for it.

You will have realised what it is you must do to get it and have recognised that ultimately your success depends on your own action.

By committing to a course of action you will not fail to enjoy success and that is what we both want for you.

I hope you have created your own DR SPACE™ and that your team in his guise will be there for you when you need them.

This is my first attempt at writing a book, a long held dream, and as you are reading this far then I guess I have achieved some success as defined by me, and that it is proof that the process works.

What matters to you is what **you** want, what **you** define as success for **you**.

I have confidence that you will move on to ever increasing success as you adopt the DR SPACE™ process.

I would always be delighted to hear of how you have used this volume to make your dreams reality.

Should you wish to know more about relationship marketing feel free to utilise the free *lifestyle questionnaire* you will find on:

www.Lifestyleboost.co.uk/success

If you find this interesting you may wonder if you have what is necessary to participate in relationship marketing.

There is a *suitability questionnaire* further on in the same site.

You may also contact me through this site if you so wish.

May you have all the success you deserve.

If you were, as we were, moved by the words of Ralph Waldo Emerson and would like to help us to help others through the our charity Give A Man A Net then visit:

www.design4success.co.uk

There is information on GAMAN and we would welcome any assistance you can give.

Whatever you do with your life identify your pillars of success and your roles.

Create your list of values and principles.

Live by the principles and values which are important to you and your whole being will benefit from the integration of the various aspects of your life.

You have the freedom already to choose and you can create the freedom to act.

design4success™**.....**

..... because it doesn't happen by accident

My very best wishes for the future.

A Candle Loses Nothing
By Lighting Another Candle

To order more copies of this book

Post a copy of this form, or write to us, with your cheque (*payable to design4success*™ **publications**) to:

design4success™ publications
The Gardens, Sisland
Loddon, Norwich NR14 6EE
United Kingdom

Tel:+44 (0)1508 528230 Fax: 0870 222 7264
email: hall@euphony.net Web: www.design4success.co.uk

Please send me .... copies of

How to stop sabotaging your success
(and get what you want guilt free)

@ £9.99 each + p&p

Postage & packing: UK: £2 per copy   Overseas: please ask for a quotation

Cheque enclosed for £.........

Name ....

Address ....

....

Telephone ....

email: ....